Foreign Direct Investment Perspective through Foreign Direct Divestment

Edited by Anita Maček

Published in London, United Kingdom

IntechOpen

Supporting open minds since 2005

Foreign Direct Investment Perspective through Foreign Direct Divestment
http://dx.doi.org/10.5772/intechopen.88720
Edited by Anita Maček

Contributors
Ignatius Roni Setyawan, Xuan Huynh Nguyen, Dinh Phi Hoang, Mohamed Salem, Paul Asquith, Stella Opoku-Owusu, Omar E. García-Bolívar, Anita Maček, Rasto Ovin

First published in London, United Kingdom, 2021 by IntechOpen
IntechOpen is the global imprint of INTECHOPEN LIMITED, registered in England and Wales, registration number: 11086078, 5 Princes Gate Court, London, SW7 2QJ, United Kingdom
Printed in Croatia

British Library Cataloguing-in-Publication Data
A catalogue record for this book is available from the British Library

Additional hard and PDF copies can be obtained from orders@intechopen.com

Foreign Direct Investment Perspective through Foreign Direct Divestment
Edited by Anita Maček
p. cm.
Print ISBN 978-1-83881-952-1
Online ISBN 978-1-83881-953-8
eBook (PDF) ISBN 978-1-83881-954-5

For EU product safety concerns:
IN TECH d.o.o., Prolaz Marije Krucifikse Kozulić 3, 51000 Rijeka, Croatia, info@intechopen.com or visit our website at intechopen.com.

Meet the editor

Professor Anita Maček is currently a lecturer of Economics at the University of Applied Sciences FH Joanneum, Graz, Austria, and the Doba Business School Maribor, Slovenia. She is also a member of the Management Board at the Union of Economists of Slovenia, editor-in-chief of the Journal of Innovative Business and Management, deputy editor of the IBS Newsletter, and a member of the editorial board of Bančni Vestnik (The Journal for Money and Banking). The focus of her research, which has been published in numerous national and international journals, is related to international capital flows, foreign direct investments, international business, cross-cultural management, smart cities, and management of cities and regions.

Contents

Preface

Since the start of the century, the world has been facing quite a substantial setback in foreign direct investment (FDI). The reasons for this could be the saturation happening in some economies (China, Central and Eastern Europe) or even disappointment, because in some cases FDI did not meet basic expectations of the receiving countries.

These events are in a way sanctioning the theoretical debate on FDI as well as the discussion surrounding mergers and acquisitions.

This book is organized into two sections.

The section on "Selected Perspectives on International Capital Flows" includes two chapters. The first chapter provides a deep analysis of how a weak business climate can cause foreign direct divestment. The chapter highlights the externalities of foreign direct divestment and suggests some ideas to overcome the related global negative impact, which is likely to be significant in the aftermath of the COVID-19 pandemic.

The second chapter in this section highlights some of the most important impacts of FDI that are subject to inverse processes later. The chapter discusses drivers of these processes and searches for different patterns, obviously often deriving outside economic rationale from the position of a developed market economy. Based on their expertise, the authors connect concrete findings of their study with possible drivers of divestment.

The section "Regional Specific Issues of Foreign Direct Investment and Divestment" consists of four chapters.

The first chapter identifies the location drivers and barriers influencing FDI in the hotel sector in selected Middle East and North Africa (MENA) countries. Results of the study show that hotel-specific variables and country-specific factors influence FDI flows in MENA countries. In addition, the study exposes taxation, level of investment freedom, and political instability as the most important barriers to these processes.

The second chapter in this section highlights the behavior of global investors in five Association of Southeast Asian Nations (ASEAN) stock markets at the industry level. The authors add important information to the topic of ASEAN capital market integration. The results of the study show that there are still differences in the level of integration between countries and industries in ASEAN, however, they also prove that the Indonesian capital market provides the greatest benefits to global investors, giving them the opportunity to utilize all Global Industry Classification Standard (GICS) industrial sectors as a reliable portfolio.

In the third chapter, the authors discuss prospects and trends in how diaspora investment can help to achieve sustainable development goals in Africa. The chapter argues that governments, financial institutions, the private sector, and the diaspora itself should view diaspora investments as part of the development financing mix, especially as part of blended finance' packages.

The last chapter of this section highlights the application of consistency fuzzy preference relations in order to select a strategy that attracts FDI in developing supporting industries for Vietnam. The authors prove that institutional policies, domestic supply capacity, human resources, and technological development, coupled with innovation, are the key criteria to consider when selecting a strategy that attracts regular FDI. Furthermore, analytical results presented in this chapter demonstrate that the best strategies for attracting FDI to Vietnam are those that motivate sustainable economic growth on an ongoing basis.

I would like to thank IntechOpen for giving me the opportunity to edit this book. I would also like to thank all the authors who responded to the call for chapters and submitted manuscripts to this book. I think that the valuable contributions included in this book are important assets for the professional community.

Anita Maček
University of Applied Sciences FH Joanneum,
Graz, Austria

Doba Business School,
Maribor, Slovenia

Section 1

Selected Perspectives on International Capital Flows

Chapter 1

Business Climate: When Weakness Means Foreign Direct Divestment

Omar E. García-Bolívar

Abstract

This chapter is about weak business climate as a cause for foreign direct divestment. The aim is to show the connection between a poor business climate and foreign direct divestment. The methodology used entails a review of the different factors of the business climate such as the ease to do business, corruption, and rule of law. A review of the UNCTAD foreign direct investment flow as compared to the business climate indicators to determine a pattern is also part of the methodology. The chapter highlights the externalities of foreign direct divestment and suggests some ideas to overcome the global negative impact of foreign direct divestment as it is estimated to be significant in the aftermath of the COVID-19 pandemic. The conclusion is that foreign direct divestments can occur for different factors, some internal and some external. Weak business climates seem to play a role in a decision to divest an investment but there is no direct correlation.

Keywords: business climate, foreign direct divestment, weak business climate, factors of foreign direct divestment, universal wealth fund

1. Introduction

Foreign direct investments (FDIs) are defined as transfer of capital from one country to other where the investor has control or a significant degree of influence on the management of a business located in the host country [1].

Foreign Direct Divestment (FDD) are defined as an adjustment in the ownership of a business that involves the partial or full disposal of an asset or a business unit [2].

The theory of economic development shows that capital is one essential piece of Gross Domestic Product (GDP) growth. The reasoning is that more FDI helps in GDP growth whereas more FDD affects the GDP growth [3].

To understand the dynamic of the FDI process and the FDD process it seems external factors play an essential role on determining the decision to invest or the decision to divest.

The literature defines business or investment climate multifold. In general, usage of the term falls into three major categories: (1) an overall measure of growth or business health in a region; (2) a set of factors believed to contribute to regional economic growth; and (3) an intangible asset in the form of a regional reputation for business friendliness and receptiveness to growth [4].

In that continuum, efficient regulations, transparency, rule of law, strong institutions, low operating costs and predictability, inter alia, are all elements that can enhance the appeal to foreign investors. That premise assumes that previous conditions need to be in place: business opportunities and a positive cost/benefit equation. However, the opposite seems to be true: poor business climates where the rule of law is weak, corruption is pervasive, costs of doing business are high and unpredictable and transparency and predictability are absent appear to deter an investment decision.

This chapter is about the business climate as a relevant factor that drives FDD. Overall the methodology followed is this: review of indicators of business climate factors. Similarly, the FDI rankings are reviewed. It is sought to find a pattern between weak indicators of business climate factors and low flow of FDI. For that purpose, some countries' rankings on doing business, corruption perception index, and rule of law index are reviewed.

The second section highlights the factors that trigger FDI. By looking at the relevant data, it is intended to stress that a better business climate ranking contributes to boost FDI flows.

The third section shows the opposite: a weak business climate fosters FDD. A country will have a weak business climate when it is ranked in the lowest range on Doing Business, Corruption Perception Index and the Rule of Law Index.

The fourth section highlights the externalities of FDD. Just as FDI is considered to bring about externalities such as job creation and productivity enhancement, a connection between FDD and loss of jobs and GDP shrinking is explored.

The fifth section makes some suggestions to mitigate the impact of FDD externalities. As this essay is written during the COVID-19 pandemic it is assumed that FDD negative externalities will be more significant globally and hence global remedies might be needed.

The sixth section contains the conclusions. Combining the analysis of the data with some empirical observations certain conclusions are reached as regards to the connection of business climate and FDD as well as to some suggestions to mitigate the FDD externalities.

The seventh section contains the references.

2. Factors that trigger FDI

Foreign direct investments (FDIs) have been considered an important tool for economic development [5].

FDIs bring about not only capital and jobs to the host countries but also enhance the economic apparatus directly and indirectly in areas such as innovation, cultural trends and even language use [6].

FDIs can be considered the historic equivalent of territory conquests. Like that possibly overextended analogy, the rationale behind the conquests are multifold. In the case of FDIs, the reason for expanding overseas can be strategic or tactical going from market reach, factory allocation, costs reduction, profit enhancement, trend following, merger, competitors chase, trademark protection, etc.

From an economic efficiency standpoint FDIs should be assumed to be conducted when the benefits exceed the costs. That does not occur all the times as some of the benefits of FDIs can differ depending on the rationale behind. In a complicated world and with FDI actors as varied as they area and with interests as varied as they could be, the benefits could be difficult to measure. For example, State owned investors could have geopolitical interests in an investment. Hence, measuring the FDI benefit merely by the existence of profit could yield a wrong conclusion.

Thus, the factors that trigger FDIs are inexorably connected to the subjacent interests. However, the data that is available measures the FDI that is homogeneous, meaning FDIs where the interests are primarily economic and where the efficiency tends to be of the essence, i.e., costs do not exceed the benefits.

Ranking of FDI recipients v. ranking in business climate factors				
Country	**FDI inflow ranking**	**Doing business ranking Total: 190**	**Corruption perception index/ranking Total: 180**	**Rule of law index ranking Total: 128**
The USA	1	6	23	21
China	2	31/ 3 (Hong Kong)	80/16(Hong Kong)	88/16 (Hong Kong)
Singapore	3	2	4	12
The Netherlands	4	42	8	5
The United Kingdom	5	8	12	13

Source: UNCTAD world investment report [7], doing business [8], transparency international [9], and WJP rule of law index [10].

Table 1.
Year 2019.

In that continuum FDI flow is linked to a positive business climate. That is, there is a correlation between a good business climate and high levels of FDI.

An analysis of a business climate combines factors extrinsic to the business that impact the success or failure of the operation. Factors such as costs and time of doing business, including permits to operate or hire, physical and human infrastructure, corruption, rule of law, governance and political stability are all part of the overall analysis of the framework of a business climate.

Countries tend to attract more FDIs when it is easier, cheaper and faster to do business, when corruption is low and when the rule of law is prevalent. **Table 1** about ranking of FDI inflow recipients show the rankings of selected countries in relevant factors of business climate. It shows that the top 5 FDI inflow recipients perform above average in some business climate factors' rankings.

A case of point is Jordan. It has been implementing significant changes to ease doing business in areas such as getting credit, paying taxes and resolving insolvencies. The Doing Business indicators, scores and rankings, have been improving in consecutive years. Inflow FDIs have increased from $1600 million to $2030 million in 3 years up to year 2017. Jordan improved its Doing Business ranking in more than 10% in 3 years (UNCTAD World Investment Report and Doing Business).

Of course, correlation makes sense when the world economy is growing, and GDP is not contracted, when there is no world economic recession and when the economic resources of the country are not limited.

3. The impact of a weak business climate

In circumstances of economic expansion there seems to be a correlation between weak business climates and low FDIs.

The empirical evidence shows that in the absence of strong business climate the host countries are more prone to attract less FDI.

For example, when the rule of law is weak FDI inflow tends to be low. **Table 2** about the rule of law index rankings and FDI inflows shows the amount of FDI attracted by countries ranked at the bottom on rule of law.

When transparency is low, FDI tends to be low. **Table 3** about the corruption perception index rankings and FDI inflows shows the amount of FDI attracted by countries ranked at the bottom on corruption.

Country	Rule of law index ranking	FDI inflow amount (in millions of US dollars)
Congo, D.R.	124	1494
Afghanistan	123	139
Mauritania	122	71

Source: UNCTAD World Investment Report [7] and WJP Rule of Law index.

Table 2.
Year 2018.

Country	Corruption perception index ranking	FDI inflow amount (in millions of US dollars)
Somalia	180	409
South Sudan	179	n/a
Syria	178	n/a
Yemen	177	-282

Source: UNCTAD World Investment Report [7] and Transparency International [9].

Table 3.
Year 2019.

Country	Economic freedom index ranking	FDI inflow amount (in millions of US dollars)
North Korea	180	N/A
Cuba	178	2134
Eritrea	177	61

Source: UNCTAD World Investment Report [7] and Heritage Foundation Economic Freedom Index [11].

Table 4.
Year 2019.

Country	Doing business ranking	FDI inflow amount (in millions of US dollars)
Somalia	190	409
Eritrea	189	61
Yemen	187	-282

Source: UNCTAD World Investment Report [7] and Doing Business [8].

Table 5.
Year 2019.

When economic freedom is restricted, FDI tends to be low. **Table 4** about the economic freedom index rankings and FDI inflows shows the amount of FDI attracted by countries ranked at the bottom on economic freedom.

When doing business is difficult, FDI tends to be low. **Table 5** about the ease of doing business rankings and FDI inflows shows the amount of FDI attracted by countries ranked at the bottom on ease to do business.

4. Negative externalities of FDD

FDIs are poverty alleviation weapons. The benefits of FDIs have been consensually accepted to be vast and broad. The range goes from job creation, cluster creation, education enhancement, food improvement, infrastructure development, tourism recognition, technology transfer and commerce catalyst up to political stability and social peace.

FDI can also fill, first, the "investment gap" by providing the much-needed capital for domestic investment; secondly, the "foreign exchange gap" by providing foreign currency through initial investments and subsequent export earnings; and finally, the "tax revenue gap" by generating tax revenues through creation of additional economic activities [12].

The contrary is also true. FDIs are defined by control of a foreign entity of a business operation beyond the borders of origin. That control usually takes the form of ownership but it is not an exclusive trait to fulfill the goal. When control of the foreign operation ceases totally or partially by change, reduction or suppression of the activity or ownership a foreign direct divestment (FDD) can be deemed to have occurred [13].

FDD can be motivated by internal reasons. Those internal reasons can be intrinsic to the whole business undertaking or internal to the local operation. They include tactical ones, such as geographic location advantage or disadvantage, financial maneuvering, business structure, or limited resources as well as strategic ones such as market reach, competitors challenge, and product development [14].

FDDs can also be motivated by external reasons. A weak business climate where rules are not respected and predictable and where doing business is not efficient might the strongest determinant to FDD (**Figure 1**).

Thus, excessive corruption which makes costs, times and procedure outcomes unpredictable can be a deterrent of FDI. However, the evidence shows that efficiency, i.e., less costs, more benefits, is the determinant external factor of FDI. The opposite, absence of efficiency, i.e., more costs, less benefits, could be a determinant factor of FDD. Hence, a correlation between difficulty of doing business and low FDI is prevalent.

A relevant example on this point is Angola. Angola has worsened its ranking and scores in the Doing Business indicators. Two of the indicators, enforcing contracts and obtaining credit have worsened during the period lapsing from the year 2015. During that period the FDI inflow have gone from $10,028 million to $ – 5732 million in 2018 (UNCTAD World Investment Report, Doing Business).

With FDD the host countries can suffer significantly in economic, social, and political terms. A fleeing capital that has been significant in terms of GDP and that

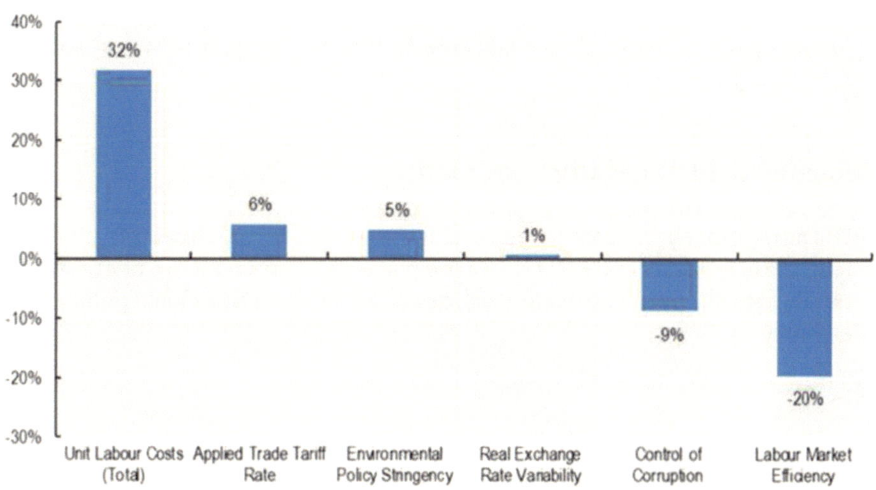

Figure 1.
The role of host country investment climate factors. Source: Borga et al. [15].

Country	FDI inflow amount (in millions of US dollars)	Refugees
Syria	N/A	5.6 million
Afghanistan	139	2.7 million
South Sudan	N/A	2.3 million
Myanmar	3554	1.1 million

Source: UNCTAD World Investment Report [7] and World Vision [16].

Table 6.
Year 2019.

Country	FDI inflow amount (in millions of US dollars)	Environmental performance index
Burundi	1	180
Bangladesh	3613	179
Congo, D.R.	1494	178

Source: UNCTAD World Investment Report [7] and Environmental Performance Index [17].

Table 7.
Year 2018.

is not substituted with other capital makes locals lose jobs, makes local small businesses vanish, and brings about losses in fiscal income, among other consequences. More significantly, the impact in the host country can also have social repercussions such as riots, violence and unrest as well as political instability.

Countries with low FDI are usually exporters of migrants. **Table 6** about FDI inflows and number of refugees shows the amount of FDI attracted by countries with most outgoing refugees.

With lack of incentives to prosper economically countries with low FDI are also more unlikely to adopt environmental friendly policies. **Table** 7 about FDI inflows and environmental performance index shows the amount of FDI attracted by countries with poor environmental performance.

Home countries are not necessarily the beneficiaries of FDD. The capital that flew away from a host country can go to another one. It might not be significant to impact in the GDP of the home country, nor to create more jobs, enhance the home country productivity or to gross up the home country's treasury. However, the global impact of massive FDDs can worsen the inequality, flows of refugees and global warming.

5. Remedies to FDD negative externalities

FDIs pursue many purposes, one of which is profit seeking. Investors might still achieve that goal after a FDD has taken place and host countries might not necessarily face all the negative externalities of FDDs if certain global policies are implemented.

5.1 ESGF

Setting up a global Environment Social and Governance Fund (ESGF) through a multilateral entity could mitigate the negative externalities of FDDs. The ESGF could endow with private capital, such as proceeds from FDD and/or open to all types of capital. The capital that is not invested in FDIs could still be beneficial to developing countries. Investors in search of profits could be benefitted, albeit without controlling the investment in a modality much more similar to portfolio investments.

The ESGF will make impact investments in different types of international business opportunities that are environmentally friendly, socially beneficial, and well governed. Home countries could play a role suggesting or encouraging owners of the FDD returning capital to devote a portion of the capital to the ESGF perhaps under certain tax arrangements, such as tax benefits to be granted to investors who devote capital to the ESGF.

The ESGF in turn could grant money to countries falling under certain economic category provided they fulfill certain objectives in environmental, social and governance policies. For example, if a country can increase its ranking in the rule of law index more than 10% every year for 2 years, the country can be entitled to participate in requests for grants from the ESGF. The grants will be disbursed on condition of maintaining certain conditions and developing programs devoted to mitigating the externalities of FDDs.

5.2 From UBI to UWF

The global economic, social and political consequences of the COVID-19 pandemic are still to be seen. It might easily happen that FDDs will occur not as a consequence of weak business climates but because of a global economic recession, lack of demand, or irrelevance of supplies. The same externalities of FDDs could be suffered by most countries.

Universal Basic Income (UBI) has been widely recommended as a measure to alleviate the needs of the poor. UBI has received recent publicity as a possible remedy to alleviate the needs of many during the pandemic crisis. The rationale behind the UBI is that people under certain conditions will receive a fixed amount of money. Once spent the UBI is evaporated and there is no legal right to it. Bluntly, it is a donation by the government.

A complementary concept might be useful: Sovereign Wealth Funds (SWF) with a more ambitious twist. SWFs are investment funds created and commonly owned by sovereign States to maximize the profits of their wealth usually but not necessarily yielding from commodities. Currently, there are more than 90 SWFs holding more $8 trillion [18].

SWFs have been highly profitable. For example, the Norway Government Pension Fund Global is the largest SWF, created in 1990 and currently holding more than $1 trillion. It has generated an average annual return of 6% since 1998 [19].

Many SWFs have been created mainly for purposes different than direct social benefits to the citizens of the owner States, such as macroeconomic policies [20]. However, in general, people receive proceeds from SWFs investments directly or indirectly, even in seemingly citizens' remote circumstances as managing the balance of payments [21].

The Alaska Permanent Fund is an example of a SWF where there is a direct benefit to the citizens as returns are distributed through a citizens' dividend program under certain conditions. It was established in the Alaska Constitution in 1976 and managed by a state-owned corporation, the Alaska Permanent Fund Corporation (APFC). It is endowed from the proceeds of oil. It distributes its returns through a citizens' dividend program. The fund currently holds over $66 billion in assets. It has paid up to $2072 in dividends.

The negative externalities of FDDs will be more prevalent in the aftermath of the COVID-19 crisis. The impact of the global recession and reduction of the demand is likely to be reflected in massive FDD. Developing countries will suffer significantly economically and socially at a minimum. The chaos of many developing countries struggling with basic needs can in turn deteriorate the business climates to further affect the flow of FDD.

Thus, inspired by the SWF, a Universal Wealth Fund (UWF or 3UF) could be established through multilateral arrangements. It could be set up to mitigate not only the effects of a surge of FDD but also the global economic and social damage post COVID-19.

The 3UF could be endowed by countries, by corporations and by NGOs. The corporations could make their contributions directly from the capital of the FDD or as some kind of tax planning tool or even as some kind of fine or penalty mitigation when they are punished or fined by multilateral entities such as the European Union.

Proceeds could be distributed directly to countries under condition that they are either invested in social projects and/or turn to the citizens in form of dividends which could be structured in terms of legal rights to which they are entitled. As opposed to UBI which are discretionary, rights to 3UF dividends can benefit large scale capitalization, financial literacy, and governance of the 3UF.

Be it as it may, the disadvantages of FDD to host developing countries could be mitigated. It was important before; it is more important in the world after the COVID-19 crisis.

6. Conclusions

FDIs are important tools for economic development. FDIs entail capital transfer to host countries which sometimes starve of funding to provide for the wellbeing of their citizens. Through FDIs many developing countries can ameliorate the impact of the poverty in the social and economic realms. Jobs are created, local business emerge, more public revenues can be collected, physical infrastructure is enhanced, human infrastructure is benefited, and the host country's branding can emerge as a favorable place to invest, among others.

The FDI process is complex as is the decision to invest. Many factors play a determinant role in FDIs. Internal and external factors of different nature can push the capital inside or outside the host country. Among the external factors, business climate plays a crucial role. The combination of external factors that is commonly known as business climate relates to all the host country's conditions that make the business easy to operate, diminish the costs and sets up in advance the rules under which the business will function. Unpredictability of rules, costs, and processes are usually contrary to FDIs. However, even in conditions of difficult, expensive, and lengthy conditions to do business, corruption, and weak rule of law, FDIs flow, albeit somehow diminished.

Countries that receive the most FDIs are ranked above average in the Doing Business indicator, Corruption Perception index and Rule of Law index. On the contrary the countries that are badly ranked in those indexes have attracted a lower amount of FDI.

The empirical evidence shows that in the absence of strong business climate the host countries are more prone to attract less FDI. That is the case with the Doing Business indicator, the Corruption Perception indicator, and the Rule of Law indicator.

It can be concluded that excessive corruption which makes costs, times, and procedure outcomes unpredictable can be a deterrent of FDI. However, the evidence shows that efficiency, i.e., less costs, more benefits, is the determinant external factor of FDI. The opposite, low efficiency, could be a determinant factor of FDD.

The correlation between weak business climates and FDD is noticeable although not determinant. As FDD decisions are dependent on internal factors of the investor as well, a conclusion on a direct relation between weak business climates and FDD cannot be reached. However, the evidence shows that absence of efficiency, i.e., more costs, less benefits, could be a determinant factor of FDD.

The impact of FDD is somehow the reverse of the benefits of FDI for the host countries. FDDs can also bring about negative externalities to the home countries under the form of migrants and deteriorated environment.

At a global level, investment funds can play a role to mitigate the impact of FDDs. A multilateral fund devoted to environmental and social projects properly governed can be established in a way that appeals the outflow capital resulting from the FDD. The profits could in turn be offered to countries that satisfy certain requirements and conditioned to be invested in projects devoted to reducing poverty or other FDD negative externalities. Similarly, an unprecedented universal Sovereign Wealth Fund could also mitigate the negative impact of massive capital mobilization from poor counties. In the seemingly critical times that will follow the COVID-19 pandemic, global policy makers need to be creative in large scale to long term sustainable solutions for all.

Conflict of interest

The author has avoided listing some countries in the rankings due to professional conflicts of interests.

Author details

Omar E. García-Bolívar
BG Consulting, Washington, D.C., USA

*Address all correspondence to: omargarcia@bg-consulting.com

References

[1] International Monetary Fund (IMF). Balance of Payments and International Investment Position Manual 100. 6th ed. 2009. Available from: https://www.imf.org/external/pubs/ft/bop/2007/pdf/bpm6.pdf

[2] Organization for Economic Co-operation and Development (OECD). Divestments by Multinational Enterprises. 2020. Available from: https://www.oecd.org/investment/Divestments-by-multinational-enterprises-Investment-Policy-Insights.pdf

[3] Dilip M, Debraj R. Readings in the Theory of Economic Development. 1999. New York University. Available from: https://www.econ.nyu.edu/user/debraj/Papers/DevReaderIntro.pdf

[4] Liesl Eathington, Aaron L. Todd, Dave Swenson. Weathering the Storm of Business Climate Rankings. 2005

[5] Hahn HJ, Gramlich L. Foreign commerce and investment in market economy countries. International Enclyclopaedia of Comparative Law. 1989;7(22):58-96

[6] Fry EH. The Politics of International Investment. New York: McGraw-Hill; 1983. p. 37

[7] World Investment Report. 2018/2019/2020. United Nations Conference for Trade and Development (UNCTAD). Available from: https://unctad.org/en/Pages/DIAE/ World%20 Investment%20Report/ World_Investment_Report.aspx

[8] Doing Business Indicator. 2015/2016/2017/ 2018/2019. World Bank. Available from: https://www.doingbusiness.org/en/doingbusiness

[9] Transparency international. Corruption Perception Index, 2019. 2019. Available from: https://www.transparency.org/cpi2019

[10] World Justice Project. Rule of Law Index, 2019. 2020. Available from: https://www.worldjusticeproject.org/rule-of-law-index/global/2019/

[11] Economic Freedom Index. 2020. Heritage Foundation. Available from: https://www.heritage.org/index/

[12] Smith S. Restrictive policy toward multinationals: Argentina and Korea. In: Case Studies in Economic Development. 2nd ed. 1997. pp. 178-189

[13] Jagersma P, van Gorp D. International divestments: An empirical perspective. Journal of General Management. 2003;**29**(1):47-67

[14] Zak K. Foreign Direct Divestment-Concept, Determinants, Major Trends: Poland in Comparison to Selected Regions in 2010-2016. 2016

[15] Borga M, Pilar IF, Monika S. Divestments by Multinational Enterprises, OECD Investment Policy Insights. Organization for Economic Co-operation and Development; 2020. Available from: https://www.oecd.org/investment/Divestments-by-multinational-enterprises-Investment-Policy-Insights.pdf

[16] Top countries refugees 2019. World Vision. Available from: https://www.worldvision.org/ refugees-news-stories/forced-to-flee-top-countries-refugees-coming-from

[17] Environmental Performance Index. 2018. Yale University. Available from: https:// epi.envirocenter.yale.edu/epi-topline?country&order=field_epi_rank_new&sort=asc

[18] Sovereign Wealth Fund Ranking. Sovereign Wealth Fund (SWF)

Institute; 2019. Available from: https://www.swfinstitute.org/ fund-rankings/sovereign-wealth-fund

[19] Norges Bank Investment Management. Government Pension Fund Global: Annual Report 2017. 2018. Available from: https://www.nbim.no/en/publications/reports/2017/annual-report-2017/

[20] Cummine A. Citizens' Wealth: Why (and How) Sovereign Funds Should be Managed by the People for the People. New Haven and London: Yale University Press; 2016

[21] Lansley S. A Sharing Economy: How Social Wealth Funds Would Tackle Inequality and Help Balance the Books. Bristol: Policy Press; 2016

Chapter 2

What Has Happened with C-B M&A Acceptance? A Follow Up Based on 2005 – 2015 Study

Rasto Ovin and Anita Macek

Abstract

Especially since 1990s when capital flows liberalization took their intensive course, also the literature on foreign direct investment and respectfully cross-border mergers and acquisitions grew. On the other hand, although it was accompanying these processes, foreign divestment attracted much less attention. Speculating about the reasons for such situation, one could stress that following the nature of the balance of payments logic foreign direct divestment was not expected. Nevertheless, these processes were present. This chapter addresses some of the most important impacts of foreign direct investment that had been a subject to inverse processes later. The authors try to confront the drivers of these processes and search for different patterns obviously often deriving outside economic rationale from the position of a developed market economy. Using their expertize the authors connected concrete findings of their study with possible drivers of divestment. According to the finding the common nominator was mixed success with the transition in transition countries.

Keywords: foreign direct investment, foreign direct divestment, cross-border mergers and acquisitions, economic effects, host economy

1. Introduction

There are several studies showing the impact of foreign direct investment (FDI) on domestic economies. Typically, studies find that inward FDI are supporting several areas of basic importance for host economy growth. Different authors put focus on different areas. First there is FDI support of access to modern technology and financial sector development - references [1, 2]. More microeconomic oriented studies found that FDI typically promotes productivity growth of an acquired firm - references [3, 4]. Macroeconomic oriented studies on the other hand bring forth FDI positive effects for the growth potential of the host economy as well as for knowledge transfer, growing engagement of local suppliers in supply chains, additional tax revenues and the better use of local services and infrastructure [5–9].

Bringing in more literature sources will provide results referring to positive effects of FDI for technology development, savings, investments and economic development and growth [10]. Furthermore FDI should promote openness to changes, improve leadership and new advanced technology [11]. According to [12]

 IntechOpen

FDI is exposed not just as a tool for increasing productivity, but also for fostering human capital development and strengthening corporate institutions.

FDI can also reduce unemployment, increase engagement of local companies in supplier and subcontractor networks, support development strategies of individual sectors, increase development potential of the economy, and develop managerial knowledge skills [13–15].

However, it is also proven that the benefits of FDI are not self-evident and that the economic effect of identical FDI can bring very different results in different countries as well as industries [16–18]. Relevant for the topic of this chapter is that proved that positive effects of FDI are not resulting in an equal effect in all branches and industries, with the same frequency and intensity. As presented by [9] the positive effects of FDI depend on the readiness of the host country to openness, and appear only after a certain period.

It is proved that the benefits from FDI increase in an open investment environment. In countries with macroeconomic stability, democratic investment regime, privatization, active competition policies, and deregulation.

However, with unfavorable conditions negative effects of FDI can occur. Reference [19] proved that FDI caused the reduction of productivity in the host country. Further FDI can reduce employment, increase concentration in the domestic market and even more it can cause the closing of domestic companies.

According to [9] FDI can lead to shrinking of the domestic stock market, anti-competitive reactions of the acquired firms, or even elimination of the domestic competition in the home market. [15] proved that one of the main threat of FDI during the last years is related to the fear of losing the national sovereignty and autonomy of the host country and consequently losing control of strategic industries.

Especially since 1990s when capital flows liberalization took their intensive course, also the literature on FDI and respectfully cross-border mergers and acquisitions (C-B M&A) grew. Although it was accompanying these processes, on the other hand, divestment attracted much less attention. Speculating about the reason for such situation, one could stress that following the nature of balance of payments logic the FDI to take an inverse course was not expected. With the theory arising already in 1980s [16], these processes were present and have been gaining on importance in later decades [17].

As foreign divestment, authors will consider reduction of assets of foreign investor in the receiving country. Authors will not discuss foreign divestment on the basis of management decisions such as changing or concentrating to core business of majority owner, change in the market positions or instability in the host country, poor performance and management, but will focus rather on vague field of general FDI acceptance in a host economy.

Authors will try to find the position of foreign divestment by the help of the data acquired by study on economic effects of C-B M&A carried out by the authors in the period between 2005 and 2015. Having certain information and experience on economies of Western Balkans authors will try to synthesize information of general attitude towards market economy and democratic development.

In this chapter, authors first summarize the results of their studies in the period between 2002 and 2015 proving predominantly positive economic effects of C-B M&A. Second part of the chapter brings the facts discussed in the literature, showing that the important part of FDI had been also subject to inverse processes later. Authors try to confront the drivers of these processes and search for different patterns obviously often deriving outside economic rationale from the position of a developed market economy.

2. Why it happened?

Basing on the theoretical paradigm of liberal concept of the balance of payments it seemed plausible that the study measuring economic effect of this form of FDI would prove the positive acceptance and sentiments of stakeholders in receiving countries. The result of authors' studies carried out in the period between 2005 and 2015 show that C-B M&A, despite some reservations in the literature [18–21], support the receiving country technological improvement and exports.

Nevertheless, at the same time also processes of divestment were taking place. According to [22] multinational enterprises divested one of every five foreign-owned affiliates over this period of time.

In the following text authors will discuss the possible reasons for divestment and will try to locate the factors that were not taken into account with authors´ study that have proved drivers of divestment sentiment.

In the last quarter of 2020 new developments in the EU saw Poland and Hungary opposing the present EU Commission threat that due to issues with (un)democratic processes in these countries (with Slovenia under present government also checking for feasibility of such course) they could be expelled from a massive economic help from the EU. This simply showed that the countries that would be beneficiaries of processes of widening of western-type democracy might have changed their view after being accepted in this noble community for which they longed for decades. No one could conclude that with pledging for acceptance in the EU the politicians as well as opinion creators were rather thinking on higher wages, access to western goods and free movement (until it suits them). Their perspective seemed to be biased towards higher standard of living without endeavor to catch up with their missing or interrupted path to a modern democratic society. The same is actually valid for the process of liberalization of capital imports. Rather than doing their homework with institutional setting and economic environment (financial markets, meritocracy, public finance transparency and accountability) which could assure FDI best contribution to the incoming countries economy, they seemingly expected (were allegedly promised) manna from heaven and are now claiming that it was rather Dans' fake gifts.

If we turn the side of the medal, we could probably conclude that there is another factor preventing host countries to be more effective with adjustment of their economic environment to the reality of liberal capital flows. The conditions in which they are supposed to open and develop their economies differ very much from the conditions that today's leading economic powers had in the time of their positioning as such. It is not difficult to conclude that the present domination of western economic model and technology was actually achieved through all kinds of their interventionism in favor of domestic economies. These were the times following first industrial revolution. Only when established as leading economies they became promotors of trade and capital flows liberalization. They are actually doing their best to impose liberal order to those, which would surely benefit from certain interventionism. The problem is that due to arrears in their (democratic and institutional) development they are not in position to carry out such policies against foreign competition without the risk of being expelled from the international trade community facing the negative consequences for their economic development and growth.

Foreign divestment must therefore be seen as a sign that with international integration and globalization also process of international economic disintegration is taking course. Opposing the dissolvent of their culture and tradition, the follower countries (countries not in first line of systemic leaders of global technology progress) no doubt have support of domestic electoral body. The solution is surely not to be find in the present economic and international co-operation model.

It needs no special proof, that "Asian tigers" have taken a different path in response to liberal capitalism. According to [23] the list of countries with highest average intelligence quotient is topped by Singapore, China, Hong Kong, South Korea and Taiwan. Being on the top by the (unpopular) criteria of intelligence quotient these societies under democratic or less democratic environments obviously succeeded with adjusting of their cultural model to the mainstream dictated by western industrial countries. Up to now, nothing else could be said apart from that, that they supply a clear proof that in favorable conditions FDI supports host country economic growth, employment, technology improvement and international competitiveness.

3. The facts deriving from author's studies

As stressed above authors base the findings on the results of their study in the period between 2005 and 2015, researching European economies that were divided in developed and transition countries and separately the ones of Slovenia and Serbia.

In the research of European economies in total 53 answers from developed countries and 38 from transition countries were analyzed. As developed countries old EU members before 2004 EU enlargement, Island, Norway and Switzerland were considered. Although there are considerable differences among them, these countries have been experiencing western type of democracy, private ownership and market economy. They are: Austria, Belgium, Cyprus, Denmark, Finland, France, Germany, Greece, Ireland, Italy, Island, Netherlands, Norway, Portugal, Spain, Sweden, Switzerland, and UK. On the other side as transition countries considered were European countries, who after World War II shared state ownership, mono-party system and central planning. Authors presupposed that these heritages should define a different need for privatization, to replace obsolete capacities in manufacturing and to develop markets and hierarchies typical for a market economy – all being normal consequences of inward C-B M&As. The countries representing this group were: Belarus, Bosnia and Herzegovina, Bulgaria, Croatia, Czech Republic, Estonia, Hungary, Latvia, Lithuania, Poland, Romania, Russia, Slovakia, Slovenia, and Serbia and Montenegro.

The results pointing to possible sentiments for foreign divestment on the side of receiving countries are stressed below.

We start with receiving countries motivation for attracting C-B M&A.

As shown in the **Table 1** the most important motives for attracting C-B M&A were the access to new markets, followed by the transition process, know-how transfer and technology improvements. External pressure on domestic policies as well as C-B M&A as a support for a better strategy of industry development did not attract much attention in relation to the motives of C-B M&A.

The attitude of expanding national economies, compared to transitional economies, where capital imports have the function of repairing domestic structural disproportions is shown with giving the higher importance to access to new markets in developed countries compared with the ranking in transition countries.

National competitiveness and the importance of development local management skills, have been considered more important motive for attracting C-B M&A in transition countries than in developed countries because the situation of catching up in this field is logically more present in transition countries.

DOI: http://dx.doi.org/10.5772/intechopen.95569

Motivation factor	Developed countries	Transition countries
External pressure on domestic politics	5,82%	7,84%
Development of local management skills	4,58%	7,84%
Lack of strategy for certain industries development	6,87%	7,84%
Part of transition process	17,46%	15,69%
Access to new market	23,50%	16,67%
Technology improvement	13,74%	12,75%
Increase of national competitiveness	12,00%	12,00%
Know-how	16,03%	14,71%

Source: [24].

Table 1.
Grounds for countries' motivation when attracting C-B M&A.

Answers also show that technology improvement is important motive for attracting C-B M&A in all countries. While in transition countries technology improvement closes the gap towards developed countries, in developed countries it is basically there for consolidation of strategic industries.

Being less motivated for entrance of foreign markets transition countries typically demonstrate themselves as closed economies in the period before the start of 1990s. Lagging behind developed countries transition countries surprisingly demonstrate that they are not as they should be convinced that the C-B M&A are also about the transition from closed economy into an open market economy.

One would also expect that meeting the western standards through C-B M&A would represent higher priority to execute external pressure on domestic politics to accomplish transition processes in transition countries.

Authors also analyzed possible threats of C-B M&A for domestic economies. Results are presented in the **Table 2**.

As it can be seen from the **Table 2** shrinking of domestic stock market was assessed as the lowest threat of C-B M&A in all receiving countries, while crowding-out of domestic industries was the highest threat for C-B M&A receiving countries.

The **Table 2** also shows that apart from 'crowding-out of domestic companies' where there was a relatively small difference between both groups of countries, other answers show quite different perspectives when assessing C-B M&A threats.

The risk of reduction in employment and decrease of competition in the home market were considered essentially larger threats in developed countries than in transition countries. Such sentiments could derive from conviction, which may be the ground for the real policy of preventing takeover bids in European developed countries: takeovers of 'national champions' may cause destabilization of labour markets. The problem of unemployment reduction because of C-B M&A is present in transition countries too but in a smaller extent, probably because C-B M&A have established themselves as one of the tools of privatization and economic restructuring, which must take place anyway.

However, in transition countries more focus is given on low pricing of sold assets and undermining of the domestic economic development strategy. These two threats received more attention in transition countries because of the huge restructuring that C-B M&A cause in this environment endangers the last positive illusions of the domestic economic development model and 'national champions' that survived the transitional process. And there is no doubt, that when they are

Threat	Developed countries	TRansition countries
Shrinking of domestic stock market	3,09%	5,88%
Crowding-out of domestic industries	25,77%	28,24%
Undermining of domestic economic development strategy	5,15%	12,94%
Low pricing of sold assets	7,22%	16,47%
Decrease of competition in the home market	20,62%	14,12%
Reduction of employment	38,14%	22,35%

Source: [24].

Table 2.
Threats of C-B M&A.

sufficiently scarce and unique, domestic assets signify a special incentive for foreign investors, which is then expected to be offset correspondingly in their selling price.

Threats of crowding-out and undermining competition through inward C-B M&A were subject to a more detailed analysis with the help of additional questions requiring detailed information on the matter. It was of special interest to us that through these questions a possible difference between expectations (threats) and experience (the cases that the respondents have registered) would arise. We have chosen the two items mentioned above, as it was expected that they would be ranked high with threats of inward C-B M&A.

In the **Table 2** above the case could be supported through the fear that C-B M&A could undermine domestic economic strategy. It should be clear that importing foreign capital should be a part of national strategy, while functioning of these investments by themselves should be treated as a step in the right direction. Without entering the reasons for such sentiment this conviction becomes relevant as soon these threats enter the domestic policy discussion with domestic critics of transition itself and trade unions. In this way, it influences politics' sentiment towards C-B M&A making it harder to the foreign investors to pursue their initial business goals and could thus pave the way for divestment.

As it can be seen in the **Table 3** the market structures in developed countries as being far more developed than those in transition countries, are obviously offering less chance to foreign affiliates to act in an anticompetitive way.

Similarly, to above risk of creating hostile environment for C-B M&A poses also the sentiment of anticompetitive behavior that was already experienced. It is surely difficult to judge when harsh competition for domestic companies was caused by the practice, normal in the West or when real anticompetitive practice was at work. This sentiment has otherwise to do with lagging institutional reforms – here in the field of competition policy.

Authors also examined professionals' assessment of media attitude towards inward C-B M&A. Results are presented in the **Table 4**.

Probable the strongest case for also existing sentiments, which may also curb divestment makes pretty inverse treatment of C-B M&A in media when considering two groups of host countries. In the **Table 4** above it is shown that C-B M&A were treated more favorably in developed countries, because inward C-B M&A in developed countries obviously face a highly developed social and economic environment with more consistent markets and financial structures and are therefore accepted more friendly in media. Further, in developed countries it is expected that they could neutralize their possible negative effects of C-B M&A more than transition countries and this can also lead to less public skepticism.

DOI: http://dx.doi.org/10.5772/intechopen.95569

Anticompetitive behavior by foreign affiliates	Developed countries	Transition countries
It has happened in several cases	11,32%	23,68%
There have been some cases when it happened	41,51%	60,53%
There have not been such behavior	47,17%	15,79%

Source: [24].

Table 3.
Anticompetitive behavior by foreign affiliates.

General treatment of C-B M&A in media	Developed countries	Transition countries
Favorable	1,89%	0%
Showing acceptance	32,08%	13,16%
Neutral	43,40%	44,74%
Not to friendly	22,64%	36,84%
Unfavorable	0%	5,26%

Source: [24].

Table 4.
General treatment of C-B M&A in the media.

The authors performed similar research by comparison of sentiments towards C-B M&A of local communities in Slovenia and in Serbia [25]. Authors were interested in the comparison between local communities in Slovenia and Serbia and they wanted to analyze the consequences of different approach with accepting change and especially international opening.

When analyzing C-B M&A threats also here results relevant for this chapter appeared. First interestingly with some threats Slovenian critical sentiments towards C-B M&A were exposed surprisingly stronger than in Serbia, regarding the fact that Slovenia is often considered as one of the champions of transition. They refer to possible reduction of employment and environmental damage, the last being nevertheless a sign of higher development level.

In the same article the explanation for such outcome is explained with the fact that at the beginning of the transition processes in Eastern Europe Slovenia was according to Economic development clear leader. This perception, however, often harmed political will to change causing arrears especially in institutional transition and was also off set in lower acceptance of foreign capital [25].

Otherwise, as expected the differences pointing at possible sentiments to support divestment are in favor of Slovenian local municipalities. So, in Serbia typically the public seems to be convinced that Serbian companies have been acquired for too low price and that foreigners could exercise unwanted influence on the local level.

To a certain extend these results coincide with the results of already mentioned study by [22]. As possible drivers of divestment sentiments here among others through statistical significance unit labour costs, trade openness, level of control of corruption labour market efficiency and environmental policy stringency was proved.

4. Conclusion

This chapter shows the summary of the results of the research [24, 25] done in European countries and separately in Serbia and Slovenia. Main positive effects as well as some threats of C-B M&A are presented. Special attention is given also to the media treatment of C-B M&A in European countries and as an important part of the FDI had been a subject to inverse processes later authors tried to connect the results of their research done in the past to these processes.

Using their expertize the authors connected concrete findings of their study with possible drivers of divestment – those coming from the policy and public sentiment in host countries were considered here. According to the findings the common nominator was mixed success with the transition process in transition countries. It proved that it would be a gap in institutional transition that prevented connection with interests of foreign investors and host country.

The results of comparison of economic effects in developed and transition countries actually enabled the insight into possible drivers of divestment. It is plausible to conclude that economic effects were focused to the beginning of transactions, while the era of investment operation dissonances could later lead to climate favorable to divestment.

For this chapter highly relevant are also findings in the source [26] that in respect to institutional distance the chances for foreign divestment are subject to an inverse U curve. This would mean that parting from lower institutional distance these chances grow, reach their peak on the border outskirts of certain institutional setting arrangements and lower when the institutional distance is bigger. Applied geographically this would be the case, which could be expected for an investor from European industrial economy. Here lower chances for foreign divestment would refer to neighboring economies and would reach their peak on the bordering belt economies – here meaning the economies of Western Balkans. Going further the Asian economies which we use as example of Asian Tigers have quite different institutional setting and thus institutional distance to the investor's country. Due to other factors mainly explainable with their flexibility the chances of foreign divestment should be reduced.

Author details

Rasto Ovin[1] and Anita Macek[2*]

1 DOBA Business School Maribor, Slovenia

2 FH Joanneum, Austria

*Address all correspondence to: anita.macek@net.doba.si

References

[1] Coe, D. T., Helpman, E., & Hoffmaister, A. W. International R&D spillovers and institutions. European Economic Review. 2009; 53(7), 723-741. DOI. 10.1016/0014-2921(94)00100-E

[2] Blomström, M., & Kokko, A. Foreign direct investment and spillovers of technology. International Journal of Technology Management: 2011; 22(5-6). DOI: 10.1504/IJTM.2001.002972

[3] Estrin, S., K. Hughes and Todd, S. Foreign Direct Investment in Central and Eastern Europe: multinationals in transition. Royal Institute of International Affairs, London, UK. 1997. ISBN 9781855674813

[4] Caves, R. E. Multinational firms, Competition and Productivity in Host-Country Markets. Economica. 1974; 41 (5): 176-193. DOI. 10.2307/2553765

[5] Liu, X., P. Siler, C Wang and Wei, Y. Productivity Spillovers from Foreign Direct Investment: Evidence from UK Industry Level Panel Data. Journal of International Business Studies. 2000, 31 (3): 407-425.

[6] Driffield, N. The Impact on Domestic Productivity of Inward Investment in the UK. The Manchester School. 2001, 69: 103-119. DOI: 10.1111/1467-9957.00237

[7] Lipsey, R. E. Interpreting Developed Countries' Foreign Direct Investment [Internet]. 2000. Available from: http://www.nber.org/papers/w7810. [Accessed: 10.11.2020]

[8] Dimelis and Louri 2002,

[9] Lin, C. H. (2008). Role of foreign direct investment in telecommunication industries: a developing countries' perspective. Contemporary Management Research [Internet]. 2008; 4(1): 29-42. Available from: https://www.cmr-journal.org/article/download/84/2047/0. [Accessed: 10.11.2020]

[10] Kumar, G. Causality between FDI and economic growth: A comparative study of India and China. Man and Development. 2011, 33 (2): 1-10.

[11] Angresano, J., Zhang, B., and Zhang. M. China's Rapid Transformation: The Role of FDI.' Global Business and Economics Review. 2002, 4(2): 223-242. DOI: 10.1504/GBER.2002.006189

[12] Arbatli, E. Economic Policies and FDI Inflows to Emerging Market Economies. IMF working paper. 2011, WP 11/192

[13] Stephan, J. Technology Transfer via Foreign Direct Investment in Central and Eastern Europe. Theory, Method of Research and Empirical Evidence. England: Palgrave Macmillan. 2005.

[14] Perez, R. P. A regional approach to study technology transfer through foreign direct investment: The electronics industry in two Mexican regions. Research Policy. 2008, 37(5): 849-860. DOI:10.1016/j.respol.2008.03.003.

[15] Maček, A., & Ovin, R. Does economic interventionism help strategic industries? Evidence from Europe. E+M. 2014; 17(3), 5-14. DOI: 10.15240/tul/001/2014-3-001.

[16] Boddewyn, J. Foreign Direct Divestment Theory: Is It the Reverse of FDI Theory? Weltwirtschaftliches Archiv [Internet]. 1983; 119(2): 345-355. Available from: http://www.jstor.org/stable/40439131 [Accessed: 10.12.2020]

[17] Brown, T. Panibratov, A. Foreign Divestment Decisions: A Theoretical Framework. St. Petersburg State University Graduate School of

Management. Saint Petersburg. [Internet]. 2016. Available from: https://core.ac.uk/download/pdf/217178973.pdf. [Accessed 12.12.2020]

[18] Basu, P., & Guariglia, A. Foreign direct investment, inequality, and growth. Journal of Macroeconomics. 2007; 29(4), 824-839. DOI:10.1016/j.jmacro.2006.02.004

[19] Tandon, Y. M&A is takeover of firms in north, economies in south [online]. Geneva: Third world network [Internet]. 2000. Available from: http://www.twnside.org.sg/title/firms.htm. [Accessed 12.12.2020]

[20] Tsang, M. and Hauck, D. Stock Markets Contract as M&A Overtakes Equity Sales [Internet]. 2007. Available from: http://www.bloomberg.com/apps/news?pid=newsarchive&sid=a7IeW7BtD0dQ. [Accessed 12.12.2020]

[21] Wyplosz, C. How Risky is Financial Liberalization in the Developing Countries? CEPR Discussion Paper. University of Geneva [online]. 2001. [Available from: http://www.cepr.org/pubs/dps/DP2724.asp. [Accessed 12.12.2020]

[22] Borga, M., Ibarlucea-Flores, P. and Sztajerowska, M. (2020). Divestments By Multinational Enterprises Accessed in December, 2020: https://www.oecd.org/investment/Divestments-by-multinational-enterprises-Investment-Policy-Insights.pdf. [Accessed 12.12.2020].

[23] Forbes. Ranked: The 25 Smartest Countries in The World. [Internet]. 2020. Available from: https://www.forbes.com/sites/duncanmadden/2019/01/11/ranked-the-25-smartest-countries-in-the-world/?sh=5c77e7e163f7. [Accessed 12.12.2020]

[24] Ovin, R., Maček, A. How beneficial are inward C-B M&A for European countries? European Journal of International Management. 2011; 4(5). DOI: 10.1504/EJIM.2010.034963

[25] Maček, A., Ovin, R., Divjak, M, Skoko H., and Horvat, T. Foreign Direct Investments' Openness in Local Communities – The case of Slovenia and Serbia. Economic Research. 2020. 10.1080/1331677X.2020.1819848

[26] Arte, P. An investigation into the impact of cross-national distance on foreign divestment. Acta Wasaensia. 2018; 401. Univesrity of Vaasa.

Section 2

Regional Specific Issues of Foreign Direct Investment and Divestment

Chapter 3

Identifying Location Drivers and Barriers of FDI Determinants in MENA Countries: Undertaking Hotel Sector

Mohamed Salem

Abstract

The study aims to examine the location drivers and barriers influencing the foreign direct investment (FDI) in the hotel sector in selected Middle Eastern and North African (MENA) countries. Data of study variables was selected from fDi Intelligence, Euromonitor International, World Economic Forum, and Datamonitor. Findings indicated a significant correlation of investor, quality, rule and law, infrastructure quality, corruption, politics, government effect, gross domestic product (GDP) growth, total tax rate, and real export GDP with FDI. However, FDI inflows were significantly determined by the level of investment freedom, investor protection, and political stability. The study concluded that investment freedom, market size, and stability of the country revealed the anticipated signs.

Keywords: barriers, drivers, FDI determinants, hotel sector, MENA countries

1. Introduction

Middle Eastern and North African (MENA) countries consist of a group of Middle Eastern and North African countries that are characterized as economically diverse regions. Among MENA countries, gross domestic product (GDP) per capita differs significantly from Qatar (46,598 US$) with the highest per capita income to Sudan, which has the lowest per capita income (719 US$). Egypt, Iran, and Turkey are the countries with the largest populations among MENA countries in terms of population size. However, GDP rate of Turkey is the largest, whereas Bahrain has the smallest GDP in terms of economic size. On the contrary, Jordan, Bahrain, Sudan, and Lebanon have the highest net of foreign direct investment (FDI) inflows, while Yemen, Syria, and Iran have the lowest net of FDI inflows in terms of GDP percentage [1]. A major challenge for resource-poor countries is represented from high inflation, importing meaningful accounts of fuel and food, while major resources of rich countries in the region are lacking. In addition, Turkey, Sudan, and Iran comprise the highest consumer price, whereas Bahrain, Saudi Arabia, Libya, and Morocco accounted the lowest consumer price in terms of the rate of inflation [2].

Financial sector development is important for the expansion and development of real estate and hotel sectors to improve inward FDI in developing and emerging markets. The most important determinants of FDI are the real estate market, market liquidity, market maturity and transparency, and institutional real estate market size [3]. Other drivers to FDI include economic and demographic factors, institutional factors, infrastructure quality, and sociocultural factors in real estate. In contrast, data availability, trading, currency, liquidity, portfolio construction, tax, and fund structuring and trading are the barriers experienced by real estate and hotel sectors [4]. However, major motivation behind the selection of real estate and hotel sectors of MENA was the paucity of empirical evidence in this region. In addition, there is very scarce academic literature in the body of context which is entirely associated with average FDI determinants. Exploratory evidence has shown interest regarding investment in specific MENA countries [5]. The availability of data in the selected countries is another influential factor.

Initially, the real estate sector is segregated into four asset classes, which include residential, industrial, retail, and office. In contrast, hotels have not been considered as a commercial real estate asset class for assorted reasons including complexity for a quick exit strategy; lack of understanding of the industry by investors, resulting from unstable cash flows; and volatility when compared to other property assets [6]. Hotel investors have different motives and barriers when venturing into these sectors. For example, hotel investors are more anxious toward the progression of the tourism industry. Government sectors are also seeking to attract capital so that they can design policies to improve and stimulate the entire investment environment and FDI, to enlarge their economies.

Previously, FDI flows were comparatively scarce in the MENA region, as compared to the European Union (EU) and other emerging and developing countries [7]. An important challenge can be experienced from several features of the MENA countries for the inward FDI performance. It is a fact that this region is highly fastened on oil, which deteriorates the economic foundation, has a high unemployment rate, has a high population growth, and portrays a deteriorated regional integration and the financial and capital markets persevere undeveloped [8]. In addition, the weight of the state in the country is still high, where the literature stresses the low rates of return on human and physical capital, the underdevelopment of physical infrastructure, and the lack of transparency in spite of the privatizations in the last years [9].

The examination of MENA institutional systems emerges to be specifically influential since a substantial number of these economies have been experiencing intense economic and institutional reforms [10]. In addition, trade relations are encouraged by the Euro-Mediterranean Partnership agreement along with the developed reduction of trade barriers. Some economies have created special regimes and liberalized investment regulatory framework for FDI. Tax and custom duty breaks, capital market reform programs, and lowering ownership limitations are included in reforms [11]. It is essential to study this subject considering the facts and the comparatively sparse empirical research on FDI in MENA countries. Therefore, this study aims to examine the location drivers and barriers influencing the FDI in real estate and hotel sectors in MENA countries.

This study has presented its novelty in different ways. Firstly, it has selected eight real estate and hotel markets in MENA countries and collected time series data during 2003–2009. The rationale behind the selection of this time period is that it provides the adequate analysis of financial development factors. These traditional factors are no longer sufficient to explain the FDI alteration; however, the quality of economic freedom is increasingly integrated into the direction of investors' choices with increasing wave of globalization. In addition, suitable techniques are applied in this study to estimate the models based on a pooled tobit model. Secondly, this study has provided multidimensional evidence on the impact of location drivers and barriers on FDI in hotel sectors practically. Moreover, Dunning's ownership, location, and internalization (OLI) paradigm is selected as a theoretical background to demonstrate the behavior of hotel foreign investors toward the selected MENA markets. Lastly, the application of economic models takes place in the emerging market. The key themes from the models are comprehensively used to cover political, sociocultural, and economic variables. This study has tried to aid governments of MENA countries to understand the drivers and barriers to sectoral-associated FDI in these markets and assist governments for reconsidering their policies by endowing specific recommendations to foreign investment policymakers.

This paper is organized as follows. The empirical literature associated with FDI and institutions, highlighting the research on the MENA countries, is reviewed in Section 2. The data utilized in the empirical study is presented in Section 3 along with some descriptive statistics on the institutional and economic variables in the MENA region. The econometric approach is presented in Section 4 along with the discussion of results. Section 5 presents the overall summary of this paper.

2. Theoretical approach to location drivers and barriers of FDI

The internationalization and traditional trade theories are embraced by the eclectic or OLI paradigm and systematized the advantages for firms that operate internationally [12, 13]. There are several benefits in selecting FDI when there are correspondingly ownership benefits such as location advantages, ownership advantages, and internationalization advantages. The significance of a firm owning assets is concerned in the ownership advantage such as exclusive productive procedures, patents, management skills, and pioneering technologies that can generate advantages in the future [14].

Location is considerable when a firm acquires from its presence in a predefined market by promoting from circumstances such as lower production, transport costs, access to protected markets, special tax regimes, and lower risks [14]. Internationalized operations, which allow a reduction in transaction costs related with risks of managing technology, can reduce market imperfections such as the imbalance of international resources allocation [12]. Therefore, the selection of a specific location is based on particular conditions that are in its preference [15]. The core objective of eclectic paradigm of Dunning to the literature was to bring forward the several complementary theories, which help in identifying a series of variables that reflect the activities of multinational enterprises [14]. The emphasis of this approach is to implement these variables for trading, for the international organization of production, and for international production. It shows that three modes of internationalization can be covered within the same analytical framework [15].

3. Related literature

3.1 Ownership-specific advantages

The OLI framework of Dunning was extended by Holsapple et al. [16] into the subject of international real estate investments. They claim that international real estate investments were hybrids of portfolio investments and direct FDI. The portfolio P subparadigm in the framework was included in the extended OLI framework for allowing the disadvantage of being international in an international environment to be comprehensively implemented. The modified framework divides ownership advantage dimension of Dunning into two subparadigms so that ownership is equivalent to ownership and portfolio in the ownership portfolio location framework.

Holsapple et al. [16] asserted that investors must assess both ownership and portfolio benefits when selecting on an investment in an international country. Further, it was demonstrated that the ownership advantages as the advantages possessed by enterprises in their host countries are transferable into international countries. It has been asserted that ownership must be taken into consideration where ownership is the advantage possessed by local enterprises to operate in the host country and claim that global investors must take into account the fixed costs of operating in a foreign environment.

3.2 Location-specific advantages

Location considerations are apparently at the core of FDI in real estate. It has been explained that real estate actors are interested in specific countries and majorly relied on a greater extent on the type of direct and indirect barriers, experienced by market actors in host countries [17, 18]. D'Arcy [18] has claimed that the business culture, institutional environment, and regulatory barriers are essential aspects when developing strategies for internationalization. Location advantages need investors for asking the where question in the OPLI extended framework in order to explore the factors such as monetary policies, host country political risks, and laws and fiscal policies. Holsapple et al. [16] claimed that location benefits must be estimated alongside the recurring costs of being international such as differential treatment in the host country or operating a long distance from the investment. Holsapple et al. [16] argued that enterprises can simply obtain passive interests in current real estate assets in the host country if they depend on portfolio advantages and the location selection is less essential.

3.3 Internalization-specific advantages

The internationalization advantage can be considered as an approach to exploit ownership by not contracting the related development activity but by objectively following it and maintaining control over it. It will be more advantageous for enterprises possessing ownership advantages to own the investment itself as compared to sell, franchise, or lease the advantage for foreign firms situated in the host country [16]. Internationalization of real estate activities is the process for determining the organizational mode by which stakeholders select to transfer capital across boundaries and intangible assets. Those intangible assets may entail human and management expertise, the reputation and knowledge of the internationalizing firm [18]. The capital transfer can be initiated and offered either from equity or debt positions, along with the financial structure related to the predefined transfer [18].

3.4 Empirical review

The location served as the central point for several researches, where it is generally highlighted as a motive for FDI. The significance of the location in FDI has been substantially supplemented by a number of studies [19–21]. Despite the immense work on the phenomena, the determination of the core location drivers for the FDI remained unknown. The study by O'brien and Williams [22] stated that the globalization and the liberalization of the national economic relations impact the significance of location which works as an important determinant for FDI. This aligns with the study of Mao and Yang [23], claiming the significance of one determinant may vary with time, as its importance declines with increase in significance of another determinant.

Theoretically, the selection of the location for the FDI has been promoted by various studies. For example, Mao and Yang [23] highlighted that FDI emerges as a consequence of the broad strategy formulated by the corporation in relation to the investment. It is based on maximizing profit while simultaneously perpetuating its global outreach. This is evident from the success of the United Kingdom, India, and Mexico for drawing hotel FDI in the periods 2005–2011 with respect to their size of the markets, taxes, and wages and degree of business regulations [24].

For Bayraktar [25], location serves as the main determinant for the FDI in terms of its investment decisions. The location drivers include land area, per capita income of the state, labor conditions, its production capacity, transportation, taxes, expenditures, as well as its agglomeration [26]. The review of the study by Yin et al. [27] illuminated that the conventional location theory, new location theory, and institutional environment regarding the labor cost, infrastructure, and market size as well as policy incentive serve as the major drivers of location for FDI.

Omoniyi and Omobitan [28] stated that the flow of FDI points toward the activities adopt with an intent to expand their profitability and competitive prospects. The activities carried out by these foreign firms are reflected as the strategies which overcome the economic gap and prevail in the domestic capital of the developing countries, simulating their economic growth. Lien and Filatotchev [29] argued that the FDI investment in terms of location is conditioned to the state capital, operations involved for its regulation, as well as parameters laid out for its repatriation of the profit and capital. Ma and Raimondos [30] further asserted that since the foreign firms are profit-oriented, therefore, the first priority is to assess return capacity of the state regardless of its host country social conditions. Location, where the possibility of capital loss prevails, is usually neglected by the firms irrespective of the industry. Falk [24] supplemented that the FDI decision is significantly related to the advantage, which the location offers to the firm. This is further corroborated by the research of Al-Shammari, Al-Halaq, and Al-Shammari [31], which adds that the advantage which the location offers serves as a catalyst for the FDI.

Snyman and Saayman [32] highlighted the characteristics of 42 host countries which influence the FDI in hotel and tourism industries. The study highlighted that political stability, health, safety, and infrastructure, i.e., airports and roads, along with factors related to cost and skills, as well as market sizes such as international tourism demand and GDP, are the main indicators of FDI location. Similarly, Brida et al. [33] highlighted the size and the past internationalization experience act as key drivers for the internationalization of Spanish hotel chains.

Phung [34] highlighted the locations' market size, trade openness, and macroeconomic stability as the prime variables for FDI. These three variables have been supported by various empirical studies, which focused on the concept of FDI [30, 34]. The explanation behind was provided by Crescenzi and Petrakos [35] stating that the investor is concerned with the return, which is in direct relation with the host country customer base size, the availability of the resources, and the implementation of trade policy.

The labor market size and its low acquisition are also regarded as the location advantages for various developing countries. Phung [34] stressed upon these factors particularly for the developing countries since it is immobile as well as region-specific. The labor incentivizes the resources for investors as they are able to locate their function in the host country lowering their cost of production. In the hospitality sector, the estimation of labor force has found to be momentous in terms of the participation made by labor, its growth, and population stock [36, 37]. Wild and Wild [38] highlighted that due to the availability of the cheap labor in Mexico, various technology- and capital-rich investors in the United States shifted to Mexico for maximizing their profitability.

Another possible driver of location was highlighted by Bénassy-Quéré et al. [39]. According to them, the variation in terms of charged tax with regard to the offered good or service significantly impacts the flow of FDI in a state. The benefits in terms of agglomeration are further supplemented by Lien and Filatotchev [29] to improve the FDI flow in the country. Another study stated that when the location is successful in attracting FDI, it paves the path and serves as a catalyst for improving future FDI. These are similar to the stated results of Phung [34] highlighting the positive link of Japanese's manufacturing plants in the United States to agglomeration when the location is being chosen.

Dunning and Lundan [14] also laid out factors in relation to the policy framework incorporating the specific policies related to the country FDI. Considering the model for general policy, it is suggested that the host country business environment should be stable in terms of its economy and political settings as well as social conditions. Reflecting upon the literature further highlighted various barriers for FDI in correspondence to the hospitality industry. Paudel and Tiwari [40] stated that the delay of approval in terms of FDI hotel serves as a major hindering block for the country hospitality sector. Evaluating the hotel and tourism industries, Bissoon [41] reported that inadequate guidelines in terms of tourism policy also impact the FDI flow in a country, particularly for its hospitality sector. Inadequate support from the regulatory institutes is also reported as the barrier for FDI.

Hayakawa et al. (2011) researched 93 countries constituting 63 developing countries and showed that the instability of the politics hinders the capability of the country for FDI inflow. Another research of Topal [42] concerning the developing country further highlighted that the reduction of the economic and political risks in terms of capital loss improves the country hotel FDI flow.

The reduction and restriction in FDI are inclusive of various factors such as legislative and regulatory frameworks, bureaucracy, protection of the investors' finances, and restrictions on the foreign ownership [43]. Another research of Azémar and Desbordes [44] proposed that regulation in the product market of the host country, which may induce additional costs for businesses, serves as an FDI barrier for their entry.

4. Methods

The study adopted a quantitative causal research design to identify and examine the location drivers and barriers influencing FDI in real estate and hotel sectors. The data was collected from eight MENA countries, which include Algeria, Egypt, Morocco, Qatar, Saudi Arabia, Turkey, Tunisia, and the United Arab Emirates (UAE) during 2003–2009 (i.e., prior the Arab spring). The selection of the host countries was indicated from the availability and accessibility of the data. Moreover, the econometric analysis was conducted for both time series and cross-sectional data using the pooled tobit model technique.

The core purpose of this study is to examine the location drivers and barriers affecting real estate and hotel sector FDI location in the MENA countries. The study has employed a panel data, which is an authentic modeling strategy including both cross-sectional and time series analyses over a short period as selected in this study. The important characteristic of panel data that differentiates it from a cross section is the same as cross-sectional units followed over a predefined time period and allowed a study of the significance of lags in behavior or the outcomes of decision-making [45]. This information can be substantial as the number of economic policies can be anticipated to have an effect merely after some time has passed. Each independent variable is lagged once a year, considering the likely form of a cause and effect relationship. Pooled tobit, fixed effect, and random effect models and pooled ordinary least squares (POLS) were anticipated to a balanced panel of appropriate data for testing the effect of the selected location drivers and barriers.

The nominal FDI flows measure the dependent variable real estate FDI as provided by the FDI market database. The level of real estate investment in each country is normalized by distributing real estate FDI by the nominal GDP of the country. This allows the author for adjusting the level of investment for the size of the economy of each country. This modification facilitates for more direct comparisons between MENA countries as the size of the GDP for each country is potentially appropriate for the extent of real estate FDI received by each country. Euromonitor International was used to derive the nominal GDP data.

Spurious results are produced by regressions performed on nonstationary time series variables. It is therefore essential for confirming that variables are stationary, which indicates that the mean and variance and probability distribution do not change over time and do not follow any patterns. An autoregressive model was used to estimate whether a time series variable is nonstationary based on a unit root test. The commonly used root tests such as Phillips-Perron and augmented Dickey-Fuller (ADF) tests lack coerciveness to differentiate the unit root from stationary alternatives. The conventional ADF-type tests of unit root further experience from the issue of low strength in order to reject the null hypothesis of stationarity of the series, particularly for short-span data.

The study variables which include real visitor export, tourist arrival, gross domestic product, overall quality of infrastructure, total tax rates, corruption, government effectiveness, regulatory quality, rule of law, voice and accountability, levels of investors protection, and levels of human development were also treated as independent variables. The data for these variables were selected from fDi Intelligence, Euromonitor International, World Economic Forum, and Datamonitor.

5. Results

This section is divided into two major results: unit root test and panel estimation. **Table 1** has summarized the results of the unit root test based on the propositions of Levin, Lin, and Chu (LLC) test. Findings have confirmed that the null hypothesis is rejected for all series investigated at their levels.

Variables	LLC test results	Conclusion
HFDIGDP	-16.5351***	I (0)
HUMANDEVELOPMENT	-1.29020*	I (0)
INFRAQUAL	-4.32190***	I (0)
INVFREEDOM	-3.55790***	I (0)
REALVEXPOTGDP	-2.44533***	I (0)
RGDPGROWTH	-6.12141***	I (0)
TAGROWTH	-5.95415***	I (0)
TOTALTAXRATE	-3.04086***	I (0)
PROTECTINVESTOR	-3.55790***	I (0)

****Significant at 1%, *significant at 10%.*

Table 1.
Unit root test results.

	HFDIGDP (−1)	TOTAL TAX RATE (−1)	REALVEXPOTGDP (−1)	TAGROWTH (−1)	RGDPGROWTH_1	HUMAN DEVELOPMENT (−1)	INFRAQUAL_1	
Mean	0.007495	40.54792	0.063554	9.871250	5.856083	0.766104	0.490380	
Median	0.004323	44.85000	0.033075	7.600000	5.328500	0.758000	0.493200	
Maximum	0.033068	76.90000	0.183237	35.95000	20.83500	0.910000	0.796320	
Minimum	0.000000	11.30000	0.001485	−18.00000	0.128000	0.583000	0.230400	
Std. Dev.	0.008347	23.16453	0.063158	10.67751	3.467567	0.094394	0.112819	
Skewness	1.315563	−0.022776	0.705193	0.412802	2.029346	−0.188557	0.135323	
Kurtosis	3.817879	1.606463	1.860656	3.810357	9.235464	1.993324	3.214573	
Observations	48	48	48	48	48	48	48	
	CORRUP (−1)	GOVEFFECT (−1)	POLITIC (−1)	PROTECTINVESTOR (−1)	REGQUALT (−1)	RULELAW (−1)	VACCOUNT (−1)	INVFREEDOM (−1)
Mean	0.348611	0.520833	0.508854	4.612500	0.731061	0.732639	0.304635	46.25000
Median	0.333333	0.500000	0.462500	5.000000	0.727273	0.791667	0.323250	50.00000
Maximum	0.500000	0.750000	0.775000	5.700000	0.954545	1.000000	0.472500	70.00000
Minimum	0.250000	0.250000	0.250000	3.000000	0.500000	0.333333	0.062500	30.00000
Std. Dev.	0.077095	0.086807	0.147541	0.935045	0.142151	0.139611	0.104689	13.62491
Skewness	0.397863	1.312546	0.206238	−0.699379	0.040110	−1.120847	−0.908529	0.243874
Kurtosis	2.418904	7.339100	2.152811	1.983307	1.998622	4.047233	3.382113	2.134145
Observations	48	48	48	48	48	48	48	48

Table 2.
Descriptive statistics for variables employed in the hotel FDI panel.

Correlation	1	2	3	4	5	6	7	8	9	10	11	12	13	14	15
HFDIGDP	1														
TOTALTAXRATE	-0.395***	1													
REALVEXPOTGDP	0.323**	0.064	1												
TAGROWTH	-0.0342	-0.2168	-0.0358	1											
RGDPGROWTH	0.238*	-0.304**	-0.0962	-0.067	1										
HUMAN DEVELOPMENT	-0.1117	0.52***	-0.0933	-0.061	-0.049	1									
INFRAQUAL	0.321**	-0.241*	0.2213	-0.064	0.44***	-0.0025	1								
CORRUP	0.369***	-0.35***	0.41***	0.0389	0.1669	-0.267**	0.244*	1							
GOVEFFECT	0.281**	-0.296**	0.122	-0.024	0.07	-0.44***	0.1852	0.0543	1						
POLITIC	0.427***	-0.54***	0.0918	-0.068	0.48***	-0.38***	0.47***	0.2075	0.329**	1					
PROTECTINVESTOR	-0.359***	-0.1763	-0.50***	0.1196	-0.0285	0.0114	-0.336**	-0.47***	-0.0958	-0.1573	1				
REGQUALT	0.372***	-0.71***	0.1007	0.016	0.1623	-0.50***	0.1924	0.340**	0.51***	0.52***	0.0136	1			
RULELAW	0.1862	-0.49***	0.44***	0.1839	0.1495	-0.311**	0.253*	0.65***	-0.1255	0.2084	-0.34***	0.328**	1		
VACCOUNT	-0.0169	0.47***	0.0386	-0.092	0.1126	0.1773	0.1028	0.2106	-0.1433	-0.0341	-0.294**	-0.48***	-0.114	1	
INVFREEDOM	0.0499	0.42***	0.242*	-0.014	-0.222*	0.37***	-0.41***	0.1588	-0.0778	-0.39***	-0.257*	-0.328**	-0.23*	0.38***	1

****, **, and * denote significant at 1%, 5%, and 10%, respectively.*

Table 3.
Correlation matrix for dependent, independent, and control variables for hotel FDI panel.

Correlation	HFDIGDP
HFDIGDP (-1)	0.391034
TOTALTAXRATE (-1)	-0.418039***
REALVEXPOTGDP (-1)	0.345872***
TAGROWTH (-1)	0.082825
RGDPGROWTH_1	0.270806**
HUMANDEVELOPMENT (-1)	-0.056115
INFRAQUAL_1	0.355238***
CORRUP (-1)	0.359171***
GOVEFFECT (-1)	0.236522*
POLITIC (-1)	0.478399***
PROTECTINVESTOR (-1)	-0.381454***
REGQUALT (-1)	0.335257***
RULELAW (-1)	0.240289*
VACCOUNT (-1)	0.010185
INVFREEDOM (-1)	0.080180

****, **, and * denote significant at 1%, 5%, and 10%, respectively.*

Table 4.
Correlation matrix (dependent vs. all independent variables) for hotel FDI panel.

5.1 Unit root test

The unit root test results indicated that the model can be anticipated regardless of any differenced variables. All the variables are stationary at level I (1), so that they are included in their actual form.

5.2 Panel model estimation

The descriptive statistics and correlation matrix have been used to calculate the absolute values of the variables in the panel model estimation (**Tables 2** and **3**).

Hotel FDI inflows have zero values, making the POLS, RE, and FE biased and inconsistent with respect to the pooled tobit test ([46], p. 616). **Table 4** shows the correlation matrix between dependent and independent variables for hotel FDI panel. Results indicate a significant correlation of investor, quality, rule and law, infrastructure quality, corruption, politics, government effect, GDP growth, total tax rate, and real export GDP with FDI.

Table 5 summarizes the results of pooled tobit regression for investigating the hotel barriers and determinants. From the findings, it is emphasized that the hotel FDI inflows are not significantly determined by control of corruption, regulatory quality, voice and accountability levels, government effectiveness, and rule of law. However, FDI inflows are significantly determined by the level of investment freedom, investor protection, and political stability (**Table 5**).

6. Discussion

The study shows an insignificant effect of control of corruption, regulatory quality, voice and accountability levels, government effectiveness, and rule of law

HFDI/GDP	Pooled tobit								
	1	2	3	4	5	6	7	8	9
Constant	−0.015938	−0.019560*	−0.026673*	−0.026624**	0.038978	−0.015241	−0.005379	−0.018302*	−0.025179**
HFDIGDP (−1)	0.036498	0.024437	0.002213	−0.012777	−0.049757	0.036856	−0.024509	−0.010593	−0.069064
TOTALTAXRATE (−1)	−0.000181***	−0.00017***	−0.00018***	−0.0001**	−0.00025***	−0.00018**	−0.00023***	−0.0002***	−0.00021***
REALVEXPOTGDP (−1)	0.055010***	0.05024***	0.05439***	0.05448***	0.046490***	0.055139***	0.071612***	0.05693***	0.037851**
TAGROWTH (−1)	3.71E-05	3.81E-05	3.10E-05	6.12E-05	5.61E-05	3.58E-05	3.62E-05	2.11E-05	1.31E-05
RGDPGROWTH_1	0.000621**	0.000591**	0.000605**	0.000530*	0.000483*	0.000619**	0.000607**	0.000495*	0.000596**
HUMANDEVELOPMENT (−1)	0.025201**	0.025477**	0.03073***	0.031677**	0.023776**	0.02503**	0.026764**	0.027620**	0.017054**
INFRAQUAL_1	0.006230	0.006678	0.005784	−0.001205	−0.006250	0.006244	0.007213	0.003966	0.022551*
CORRUP (−1)		0.009782							
GOVEFFECT (−1)			0.013991						
POLITIC (−1)				0.017354*					
PROTECTINVESTOR (−1)					−0.00805**				
REGQUALT (−1)						−0.000622			
RULELAW (−1)							−0.014402		
VACCOUNT (−1)								0.016666	
INVFREEDOM (−1)									0.000241**
No. of observation	48	48	48	48	48	48	48	48	48
Left censored obs	5	5	5	5	5	5	5	5	5
Uncensored obs	43	43	43	43	43	43	43	43	43
Log likelihood	150.5809	150.7858	151.1739	152.1154	152.617	150.5825	151.5974	151.6004	153.1897
LR chi square	26.86752	27.27717	28.05343	29.93649	30.93959	26.87071	28.9005	28.90633	32.08509

HFDI/GDP	Pooled tobit								
	1	2	3	4	5	6	7	8	9
Prob>Chi square	0.0004	0.0006	0.0005	0.0002	0.0001	0.0007	0.0003	0.0003	0.0001

, **, and * denote significance at 10%, 5%, and 1%, respectively.*

Table 5.
Determinants of hotel FDI (pooled tobit).

but a significant effect of level of investment freedom, investor protection, and political stability on hotel FDI inflows. The findings indicate a positive but insignificant effect of corruption on the FDI inflows, which reveals that the role of corruption toward hotel FDI decisions is not critical.

Also, a negative and insignificant effect of regulatory quality on hotel FDI in MENA countries at 5% level of significance is identified, indicating it an unimportant determinant for hotel-related FDI decisions. Findings further indicated a negative and insignificant effect of rule of law on hotel FDI in MENA countries at 5% level of significance, indicating it an unimportant determinant for hotel-related FDI decisions. However, the findings have shown a positive but insignificant effect of voice and accountability on hotel FDI in MENA countries at 5% level of significance, indicating it an unimportant determinant for hotel-related FDI decisions. In contrast, findings provided a positive and significant effect of level of investment freedom on hotel FDI in MENA countries at 5% level of significance, referring it an ineffective determinant for hotel-related FDI decisions.

In this regard, Falk [24] indicated a positive but insignificant effect of corruption and tax rates on the hotel FDI projects in 104 host countries from 2005 to 2011. Nguyen et al. [47] have indicated a positive and significant impact of corruption on the FDI inflows in the service sector in Vietnam. The study has observed that the extent of corruption in Vietnam is lagging behind the country in terms of market institutions and the legal systems. In addition, Shah and Azam [48] also found the insignificant influence of corruption index on FDI inflows in MENA countries from 2003 to 2016.

Similarly, the present study showed a positive and insignificant effect of government effectiveness on hotel FDI, which indicates an unimportant determinant in hotel FDI decisions. In this regard, Shah and Afridi [49] have found a significant impact of government effectiveness on hotel FDI in SAARC countries from 2006 to 2014. Subramanian and Subramanian [50] showed a significant impact on government effectiveness in the service sector in India. It further indicated that the steps attempted by the government are effective in short run but can be successful in the long run if exporters concentrate on value addition, which offsets the rising domestic interest rates, and market development and calculated measures of restrictions are taken.

A positive and significant impact of political stability has been found on hotel FDI inflows, which shows that political stability acts as a core determinant in attracting hotel-associated investments in specific markets. Mao and Yang [23] found a significant and positive impact of political stability on FDI inflows in Chinese domestic hotels. It further provided significant spillovers in domestic hotels of Eastern and Western China. Findings provided in the study of Tekin [51] indicated the negative and indirect effect of political instability on FDI inflows of Russian and Turkish tourism industries. Maclean et al. [52] outlined that macro-political instability universalizes the growth of multinational hotel industry. The study provided that the postwar globalization and its associated discourses demonstrate the ideology of the hotel industry.

The panel model estimation showed a negative but significant effect of the strength of investor on the hotel FDI inflows at the 5% level of significance. There is empirical evidence in the hotel industry which shows a positive relationship between investors and FDI inflows. In addition, the study of Nam [53] indicated a significant effect of the strength of investors on the hotel FDI inflows by revealing a positive association between private and public hotels. The interest of investors toward the FDI inflows in Cambodian hotels is developed from the value-added benefits of each type of hotel investment. Kumar [54] on the other hand outlined a positive and significant impact of the strength of investors toward maintaining budget hotels and quality of hotel services.

7. Limitations

The study presented several limitations based on the model and findings. Firstly, it used data on an aggregate level, which augments the possibility that some information is lost during the data collection and transformation process. Secondly, only annual time series data is used to compute the panel models. Thirdly, data has been extracted from 2003 to 2009, which indicates doubts whether a vigorous econometric analysis can be conducted. It was also not possible for expanding more on the qualitative data end since the study period was based on only 6 years. However, this is an opportunity for future researchers to collect more primary data from policymakers, hotel markets intermediaries, and foreign investors. Lastly, public and private agencies have been used as potential sources to measure the accuracy of the data and, therefore, challenge the accuracy of such data. However, findings obtained through such data have provided significant empirical evidence for hotel investors and markets.

8. Conclusion

The study was aimed to investigate the location drivers and barriers of FDI determinants in MENA countries within the hotel sectors. In this regard, findings obtained from the econometric analysis of hotel FDI inflows have shown that hotel sector-specific variables and country-specific factors are influencing the FDI inflows in MENA countries, though the findings of the study are somewhat unsupportive. For instance, hotel FDI values are insignificant for FDI flows for the selected MENA countries, whereas investment freedom, market size, and stability of the country revealed the anticipated signs. In addition, the study showed an opposite sign of the investor protection, indicating that hotel investors are reducing such risks significantly and accomplishing a high extent of control through specific contractual agreements.

It further indicated three common barriers, which include taxation, level of investment freedom, and political instability. These barriers have explained why MENA countries attract hotel FDI at the least extent than to other countries at a similar stage of development. The level of investment freedom is found to be a significant and important barrier in explaining hotel-related FDI. Terrorism, political instability, and violence are shown as important barriers in restricting MENA countries toward hotel FDI inflows. Lastly, taxation also restricts hotels in MENA countries to attract toward FDI inflows.

9. Recommendations

Several recommendations are proposed for future research in this context. Firstly, it is recommended that the current research should be extended to investigate the influence of FDI determinants on economic growth of MENA countries. It will be of beneficial interest to indicate the significance of hotel sector to explain the wider economy and whether governments are making significant efforts to acquire explicit advantage for hotel sector as part of their economic growth. Secondly, it is recommended to undertake different regions or countries such as South East Asia or Eastern Europe. This may include hotel-related FDIs. Data sources could vary though, especially for FDI-related variables. Concerning independent variables, the current study already tried pragmatically a number of variables for the first time and thus suggests that variables from this study as well as other variables will be interesting to be empirically tested.

Author details

Mohamed Salem
Australian College of Kuwait, Kuwait City, Kuwait

*Address all correspondence to: msalem@ack.edu.kw

References

[1] Binkhamis M. Barriers and Threats to Foreign Direct Investment (FDI) in Saudi Arabia: A Study of Regulatory, Political and Economic Factors. PhD Thesis. De Montfort University; 2016

[2] Miniesy RS, Elish E. Is MENA different? An investigation of the host country determinants of Chinese Outward foreign direct investment. In Economic Research Forum Working Papers (No. 1024). RePEc (Research Papers in Economics); 2016

[3] Shah MH. Financial development and foreign direct investment: The case of Middle East and North African (MENA) developing nations. University of Haripur Journal of Management. 30 October 2016;**1**(2):93-109

[4] Anyanwu JC, Yameogo ND. What drives foreign direct investments into West Africa? An empirical investigation. African Development Review. 2015;**27**(3):199-215. DOI: 10.1111/1467-8268.12141

[5] Gharaibeh AMO. The determinants of foreign direct investment-empirical evidence from Bahrain. International Journal of Business and Social Science. 2015;**6**(8):94-106

[6] Salem M, Baum A. Determinants of foreign direct real estate investment in selected MENA countries. Journal of Property Investment & Finance. 2016;**34**(2)116-142

[7] Hisarciklilar M, Kayam S, Kayalica M. Locational Drivers of FDI in MENA Countries: A Spatial Attempt. 2006

[8] Chauvin N. FDI Flows in the MENA Region: Features and Impacts. Institute for Emerging Market Studies (IEMS), Moscow School of Management. Vol. 13. 2013

[9] Caetano J, Galego A. FDI in the European Union and MENA countries: Institutional and economic determinants. In: CEFAGE-UE Working Paper. RePEc (Research Papers in Economics); 2009. p. 9

[10] Brewer TL. Foreign direct investment in emerging market countries. In: The Global Race for Foreign Direct Investment. Berlin, Heidelberg: Springer; 1993. pp. 177-203

[11] Ahmed NF, Mei JL, Iman AH. The determinants of ASEAN countries attractiveness to foreign direct investment in real estate. In: 21st Annual Pacific Rim Estate Societies Conference, Kuala Lumpur, Malaysia. 2015. pp. 18-21

[12] Dunning JH. Theories and Paradigms of International Business Activity: The Selected Essays of John H. Dunning. UK: Edward Elgar; 2002

[13] Faeth I. Determinants of foreign direct investment—A tale of nine theoretical models. Journal of Economic Surveys. 2009;**23**(1):165-196

[14] Dunning JH, Lundan SM. Institutions and the OLI paradigm of the multinational enterprise. Asia Pacific Journal of Management. 2008;**25**(4):573-593. DOI: 10.18356/43ce1fe7-en

[15] Ietto-Gillies G. Dunning's Eclectic Framework. Edward Elgar Publishing: Transnational Corporations and International Production; 2005. pp. 112-121

[16] Holsapple E, Ozawa T, Olienyk J. Foreign direct and portfolio investment in real estate: An eclectic paradigm. Journal of Real Estate Portfolio Management. 2006;**12**(1):37-47

[17] Baum A, Murray C. Understanding the barriers to real estate investment in developing countries. In: Proceedings of the International Real Estate Research

Symposium (IRERS). Kualar Lumpur, Malaysia; 27-29 April 2010

[18] D'Arcy E. The evolution of institutional arrangements to support the internationalisation of real estate involvements: Some evidence from Europe. Journal of European Real Estate Research. 2009;**2**:280-293

[19] Aleksandruk P, Forte R. Location determinants of Portuguese FDI in Poland. Baltic Journal of European Studies. 2016;**6**(2):160-183. DOI: 10.1515/bjes-2016-0017

[20] Buckley PJ, Yu P, Liu Q, Munjal S, Tao P. The institutional influence on the location strategies of multinational enterprises from emerging economies: Evidence from China's cross-border mergers and acquisitions. Management and Organization Review. 2016;**12**(3):425-448. DOI: 10.1017/mor.2016.21

[21] Che Y, Du J, Lu Y, Tao Z. Institutional difference and FDI location choice: Evidence from China. 2017. Available from: https://ideas.repec.org/p/pra/mprapa/77158.html

[22] O'brien R, Williams M. Global Political Economy: Evolution and Dynamics. Basingstoke: Palgrave, Macmillan; 2013

[23] Mao ZE, Yang Y. FDI spillovers in the Chinese hotel industry: The role of geographic regions, star-rating classifications, ownership types, and foreign capital origins. Tourism Management. 2016;**54**:1-12. DOI: 10.1016/j.tourman.2015.10.011

[24] Falk M. A gravity model of foreign direct investment in the hospitality industry. Tourism Management. 2016;**55**:225-237. DOI: 10.1016/j.tourman.2016.02.012

[25] Bayraktar N. Foreign direct investment and investment climate. Procedia Economics and Finance. 2013;**5**:83-92. DOI: 10.1016/s2212-5671(13)00013-0

[26] Li S, Angelino A, Yin H, Spigarelli F. Determinants of FDI localization in China: A county-level analysis for the pharmaceutical industry. International Journal of Environmental Research and Public Health. 2017;**14**(9):985. DOI: 10.3390/ijerph14090985

[27] Yin F, Ye M, Xu L. Location determinants of foreign direct investment in services evidence from Chinese provincial-level data. In: LSE Asia Research Centre Working Papers. 2014

[28] Omoniyi BB, Omobitan OA. The impact of foreign direct investment on economic growth in Nigeria. International Research Journal of Finance and Economics. 2011;**73**:133

[29] Lien YC, Filatotchev I. Ownership characteristics as determinants of FDI location decisions in emerging economies. Journal of World Business. Elsevier. 2015;**50**(4):637-650. DOI: 10.1016/j.jwb.2014.09.002

[30] Ma J, Raimondos P. Competition for FDI and Profit Shifting. CESifo Working Paper Series, 5153; 2015

[31] Al-Shammari N, Al-Halaq S, Al-Shammari D. Testing the FDI hypothesis of location advantage in the case of Kuwait. Journal of Applied Business Research (JABR). 2016;**32**(2):597-606. DOI: 10.19030/jabr.v32i2.9598

[32] Snyman JA, Saayman M. Key factors influencing foreign direct investment in the tourism industry in South Africa. Tourism Review. 2009;**64**(3):49-58

[33] Brida JG, Driha OM, Ramón-Rodríguez AB, Scuderi R. Dynamics of internationalisation of the hotel industry: The case of Spain.

International Journal of Contemporary Hospitality Management. 2015;**27**(5):1024-1047

[34] Phung H. Determinants of FDI into Developing Countries. Mark A Endowment Summer Research fund in Economics; 2016

[35] Crescenzi R, Petrakos G. The European Union and its neighboring countries: The economic geography of trade, foreign direct investment and development. Environment and Planning C: Government and Policy. 2016;**34**(4):581-591. DOI: 10.1177/0263774x16642640

[36] Shahmoradi B, Baghbanyan M. Determinants of foreign direct investment in developing countries: A panel data analysis. Asian Economic and Financial Review. 2011;**1**(2):49

[37] Williams K. Foreign direct investment in Latin America and the Caribbean: An empirical analysis. Latin American Journal of Economics. 2015;**52**(1):57-77. DOI: 10.7764/laje.52.1.57

[38] Wild and Wild. International Business: The Challenges of Globalization. 6th ed. Pearson Education Limited: Essex; 2012

[39] Bénassy-Quéré A, Fontagné L, Lahrèche-Révil A. How does FDI react to corporate taxation? International Tax and Public Finance. 2005;**12**(5):583-603. DOI: 10.1007/s10797-005-2652-4

[40] Paudel RC, Tiwari GP. Barriers and solution for better investment climate in Nepal. International Journal of Humanities and Social Science. 3. 2018

[41] Bissoon O. Corporate social responsibility in Mauritius: An analysis of annual reports of multinational hotel groups. Asian Journal of Sustainability and Social Responsibility. 2018;**3**(1):2. DOI: 10.1186/s41180-017-0017-4

[42] Topal MH. The effect of country risk on foreign direct investment: A dynamic panel data analysis for developing countries. Journal of Economics Library. 2016;**3**(1):141-155

[43] Kalinova B, Palerm A, Thomsen S. OECD's FDI Restrictiveness Index: 2010 Update (No. 2010/3). Paris, France: OECD Publishing; 2010

[44] Azémar C, Desbordes R. Short-run strategies for attracting foreign direct investment. The World Economy. 2010;**33**(7):928-957. DOI: 10.1111/j.1467-9701.2010.01226.x

[45] Wooldridge JM. Econometric Analysis of Cross Section and Panel Data. Cambridge, MA: MIT Press; 2002. p. 108

[46] Gujarati D. Basic Econometrics. New York: McGraw Hill; 2009

[47] Nguyen TLA, Saleh AS, Safari A. The impact of government policies on FDI decision of multinational corporations: An application to the Vietnamese service industry. International Journal of Economics and Business Research. 2018;**15**(2):204-222. DOI: 10.1504/ijebr.2018.089687

[48] Shah MH, Azam A. Financial development and investors location choice in the Arab world. International Journal of Business Studies Review. 2018;**4**(1):58-74

[49] Shah MH, Afridi AG. Significance of good governance for FDI inflows in SAARC countries. Business & Economic Review. 2015;7(2):31-52. DOI: 10.22547/ber/7.2.2

[50] Subramanian S, Subramanian V. Foreign direct investment for indian rupee appreciation a lesson at the right time. Journal of Advances in Business Management. January-March 2017;**3**(01). eISSN-2395-7441/pISSN-2395-7328

[51] Tekin E. The impacts of political and economic uncertainties on the tourism industry in Turkey. Mediterranean Journal of Social Sciences. 2015;**6**(2S5):265. DOI: 10.5901/mjss.2015.v6n2s5p26

[52] Maclean M, Harvey C, Suddaby R, O'Gorman K. Political ideology and the discursive construction of the multinational hotel industry. Human Relations. 2018;**71**(6):766-795. DOI: 10.1177/0018726717718919

[53] Nam S. Assessing the impacts of foreign direct investment (FDI) on local skills development: The hotel industry in Siem reap [doctoral dissertation]. Cambodia: Auckland University of Technology; 2018

[54] Kumar K. Determinants of growth and challenges in hotel industry: A study of budget and luxury segments of hotel business in India. Clear International Journal of Research in Commerce & Management. 2016;**7**(3):24-31. DOI: 10.4172/2169-0286.1000169

Chapter 4

Behavior of Global Investors in Five ASEAN Stock Markets in the Industry Level

Ignatius Roni Setyawan

Abstract

When the capital markets in ASEAN are integrated, global investors can still pursue the benefits of international diversification more than in the country level but in also in the industry level. The intended international diversification is diversification between industries. To implement this diversification between industries, measurement tools are needed to determine the benefits of international diversification directly. The intended instrument tool is a correlation which in this study uses country level correlation and industry level correlation. In order for these two correlations to be effective, it is necessary to make a hypothesis test to find if there is a difference in the level of integration between country and industry levels in ASEAN. To analyze industry level correlations, Equally Weighted and Value Weighted estimation procedures are required to test the construction of industry sector sample data according to GICS. The results show that there are differences in the level of integration between country and industry levels in ASEAN and the implication that the Indonesian capital market provide the greatest benefits and global investors could utilize all GICS industrial sectors as a reliable portfolio. The practical implications of these final result is choosing countries and industries are the best for the portfolios.

Keywords: inter-industry diversification benefit in ASEAN, country and industrial level correlation, Global Industry Classification Standard, global investors

1. Introduction

Until now ASEAN stock exchanges are still a mainstay of potential portfolios for global investors. The main consideration is due to the higher yield offered than other regional exchanges. The reason for this high yield offer is due to high banking interest rates in ASEAN. In the development of international diversification studies, it turns out that global investors are also concerned with aspects of the industry besides of course high returns. The classic study from Roll [1] states that when the benefits of international diversification cannot be achieved due to the process of increasing the integration of capital markets in one region, the choice of diversification between industries becomes more relevant. This is based on the idea that the process of capital market integration is more rapid at the country level and will be less rapid at the industry level. Several other researchers stated that industrial factors are more non-systematic than state factors. Since the classic study of Roll [1] states that industrial factors have an important role in the effectiveness of international diversification, many researchers such as Ratner and Leal [2], Richard [3], Hwang and Sitorus [4], Do et al. [5], and Chen et al. [6] began to use industry data such as Global Industry Classification Standard (GICS). According to Menchero and Morozov [7] GICS has been more globalized than other industry standards since it was handled by Morgan Stanley Capital International (MSCI).

This study intends to measure the benefits of international diversification on the ASEAN stock exchanges by using unconditional correlations of the return of the five market indices in ASEAN including KLCI (Malaysia), STI (Singapore), Thailand (SET), Philippines (PSI), and IHSG (Indonesia), respectively, with the return of MSCI. The type of unconditional correlation of each index with MSCI is seen to be stronger than the correlation between the indexes of each ASEAN country itself and the VAR and VECM cointegration analysis that has been used by Endri [8], Robiyanto and Ernayani [9], and other researchers. The advantage of this correlation is that it is able to regulate the magnitude of the correlation number lower than the correlation among ASEAN countries' own indexes. The low magnitude of correlation supports the potential benefits of international diversification in ASEAN. VAR and VECM cointegration analysis is only able to prove the presence or absence of capital market integration and is still unable to calculate the benefits of international diversification.

What is new in this study is the use of unconditional level industry correlations in each ASEAN country. The use of industry level correlations to reaffirm the argument of Click and Plummer [10] about international diversification between industries is more effective in ASEAN than international diversification between countries. This is because ASEAN capital markets have been integrated since the last 20 years. Industry unconditional level correlations are calculated in equally weighted (EW) and value-weighted (VW), both with local currency (LOC) and USD referring to the correlation estimation procedure from Kim [11]. The use of EW and VW will be able to produce different levels of correlation between industries in the five ASEAN exchanges and will further determine the level of benefit of diversification among different industries. The use of EW and VW is also in line with the research conducted by Vo et al. [12], which is based on the research of Nguyen [13].

Thus the main problem of this study is "there are still differences in the level of integration of capital markets at the country and industry levels in the five ASEAN capital markets." The different levels of integration show the different benefits of international diversification at the country and industry levels. This issue is representative of studies from Setyawan [14] and Setyawan and Wibowo [15] which emphasize the importance of correlation as a measure of capital market integration as well as the benefits of international diversification rather than cointegration analysis, namely, vector autoregression (VAR) and vector error correction model (VECM).

The reason for setting the observation period from 2006 to 2009 in this study is because it is related to my study period in a doctoral program several years ago, at which time I was asked by my supervisor to calculate the variable of level of intra-industry competition as measured by the entropy index of Ruefli [16]. The use of the entropy index in the study of capital market integration is to my knowledge that I have just done it and it must be admitted that it has made an extraordinary contribution because in empirical testing in Setyawan and Wibowo [15], the entropy index variable has a significant influence on the level of capital market integration both by using unconditional correlation by Pearson and dynamic conditional correlation by Engle [17]. My study in this book chapter is actually the initial part of my dissertation research [14]. The calculation of correlations between industries by utilizing the GICS database is very useful for the calculation of the entropy index. The entropy index calculation requires creating a mock database in GICS to be effective (see Setyawan [14] and Setyawan and Wibowo [15]). So the time to calculate the entropy index will be very long and tiring.

2. Theoretical review

2.1 Benefits of international diversification with industrial level correlations

The benefits of international diversification for industry level correlations are measured by Pearson correlation referring to the studies of Vo et al. [12], Nguyen [13], Setyawan [14], Luzey and Zhang [18], and Dutt and Mihov [19]. They formulate the unconditional level industry correlations, namely:

$$\varrho(R_{ijt}, R_{wt}) = \frac{\text{Cov } R_{ijt}, R_{wt}}{\sigma R_{ijt} * \sigma R_{wt}} \tag{1}$$

where:
$\varrho(R_{ijt}, R_{wt})$ = R_{ijt} and R_{wt} correlation with unconditional correlation (Pearson)
Cov R_{ijt}, R_{wt} = R_{ijt} and R_{wt} covariance
σR_{ijt} = standard deviation of R_{ijt} (industrial return i in country j at time t)
σR_{wt} = R_{wt} standard (international index return (world) w at time t)
$*$ = multiplication symbol (sign)
Some steps to determine ϱ (R_{ijt}, R_{wt}) are as follows:

First, calculate R_{ijt}, which is the difference in the close price indices of industry i for each country j when t and t-1. Since the period t is monthly in 1 year, then it should also be the dividend factor of each company (1, 2, 3, 4, 5 ... n) incorporated in industry i also included in the calculation component of R_{ijt}.

Second, calculate R_{wt}, the difference between the MSCI international index at time t and t-1.

Third, do the correlation calculation process between R_{ijt} and R_{wt} with σ as the standard deviation or variant root for R_{ijt} and R_{wt}, respectively.

Technically measuring industrial level unconditional correlation (UCC) is used in the EW and VW categories. Kim's study [11] provides a measure of stock portfolio returns for one industry sector in the United States Industrial Classification (USIC) category. Determination of EW is done by utilizing the multiplier 1/N for $\sum$ Rij, while the determination of VW is done by using the multiplier factor Rijt $*$ Xi, where Xi is the proxy market capitalization of an industry.

This market capitalization calculation will have an impact as an industry effect on the determinant return model, whereas fixing the local and USD exchange rates at the industrial level UCC justifies whether the effect of exchange rates on international diversification between countries will also apply to diversification between industries. This is because a study from Eun and Rescnick [20] found that when the local exchange rate is converted to USD, the correlation between R_{ijt} and R_{wt} will weaken.

Based on formula 1 and Kim's [11] and Vo et al. [12] studies, the unconditional industry level correlations such as EW can be measured with this formula:

$$\varrho\left[E(R_{ijt})_{EW}, R_{wt}\right] = \frac{\text{Cov}\left[E(R_{ijt})_{EW}, R_{wt}\right]}{\sigma E(R_{ijt})_{EW} * \sigma R_{wt}} \tag{2}$$

will be obtained.

2.2 Benefits of international diversification with country level correlations

As suggested by Nguyen [13] and Vo et al. [12], when applied at the country level, the formulation ϱ (R_{ijt}, R_{wt}) in part 1 has been modified, namely, the component R_{ijt} to R_j (state market index return j at time t). The importance of estimation ϱ (R_{jt}, R_{wt}) is to prove the hypothesis of differences in the level of integration at the country level. Unlike the R_{ijt} which is composed of stock portfolios according to the EW and VW categories, it is not the case for R_{jt}, so it is formulated as follows:

$$\varrho(R_{jt}, R_{wt}) = \frac{\text{Cov } R_{jt}, R_{wt}}{\sigma R_{jt} * \sigma R_{wt}} \tag{3}$$

Based on formulas 1, 2, and 3, it can be concluded that the lower the value of covariance between R_{ijt} and R_{wt} as well as R_{jt} and R_{wt}, the lower the correlation between industry level and country level. Where this will mean the higher the benefits of international diversification that occurs both diversification between industries and between countries.

3. Research method

3.1 Unit of analysis and data

This study uses analysis units of several market indexes in five ASEAN stock exchanges consisting of KLCI (Malaysia), STI (Singapore), IHSG (Indonesia), SET (Thailand), and PSI (Philippines). From the five market indices, each return will be estimated which will be correlated with the MSCI return index to determine the degree of integration in the ASEAN capital market with the MSCI index. The type of correlation, the Pearson correlation, is unconditional because it can eliminate the pattern of volatility clustering between the indexes of five ASEAN countries and MSCI. The pattern of volatility clustering tends to lead to high levels of correlation which will actually reduce the benefits of international diversification.

The index data of the five ASEAN countries were taken from Bloomberg from January 1, 2006, to December 31, 2009, while the MSCI index data was taken from the MSCI website www.mscibarra.com for the period January 1, 2006, to December 31, 2009 as well. MSCI industry data consists of 10 industrial sectors, namely, oil and gas (OG), industrial goods (IG), basic materials (BM), consumer goods (CG), health care (HC), financial institution (FI), service goods (SG), technologies (TC), property and real estate (PR), and utilities and telecommunication (UT), which are taken from www.mscibarra.com, and an index of each industry is derived from the construction of company data as a member of the industry. As stated at the beginning of writing this book chapter, the selection of 2006–2009 data regarding my dissertation research period which has the main interest proves the effectiveness of the entropy index as the main determinant of the level of capital market integration in ASEAN. The study results will complement the various findings from the Hwang and Sitorus study (2014), namely, the consistency of the use of 10 types of industries in the GICS database by equally weighted and value-weighted for the estimation of industry level correlations.

3.2 Analysis tool

Referring to the problem that there are still differences in the level of integration of capital markets at the country and industry levels in the five ASEAN capital markets, the analysis tool is the F-test (ANOVA) with specifications according to Setyawan [14] as follows:

1. H0 test at country level integration j = 1, 2, 3, 4, 5 for the five ASEAN countries, namely:

    a. H0: μ1 = μ2 = μ3 = μ4 = μ5 (μ is the average level of integration at country level).

    H1: one or more of the μ is different or not the same as the other μ.

    b. Level of significance: 1-α = 95%, and F-test is done with the inference process; if F-test > F-table or p-value <0.05, then H0 is rejected.

    c. If H1 is accepted, it means that there is a difference in the level of integration in the ASEAN exchange.

2. The H0 test at the industry level integration i = 1.2, up to 10 for the 10 GICS industries, namely:

    a. H0: μ1 = μ2 = μ3 = μ4 = μ5 … .. = μ10 (average industrial level integration level).

    H1: one or more of the μ is different or not the same as the other μ.

    b. Level of significance: 1-α = 95%, and F-test is done with the inference process; if F-test > F-table or p-value <0.05, then H0 is rejected.

    c. If H1 is accepted, it means that there are differences in the level of sectoral integration of 10 GICS industries in 5 ASEAN countries.

4. Result analysis

4.1 Benefits of international diversification with country level correlations

In the section below, the unconditional correlation values vary between each index return of ASEAN countries and MSCI returns. The analysis in **Table 1** is done in local currencies and USD. Based on the observation in **Table 1**, it appears that Indonesia has the weakest negative correlation, which indicates the greatest benefit of international diversification. On the contrary, for the Philippines, even though it has a correlation of close to zero, it cannot be categorized as providing the benefit of a large international diversification considering that the Philippines capital market has the most isolated nature compared to 4 other ASEAN countries.

Based on **Table 1**, it can be stated generally that unconditional correlations in five ASEAN countries between the index returns of each country and MSCI returns are still much lower than the correlation returns between index pairs of each ASEAN country which confirm the potential gap of diversification benefits internationally in ASEAN that can be utilized by global investors. Based on the opinions of Piumsombun [21], Hwang and Sitorus [4], and Do et al. [5], the ASEAN countries which have smaller values of standard deviations than that of the mean for each unconditional correlation will have the potential benefits of international diversification. If you see **Table 1**, the ASEAN countries are Singapore (LOC and

ASEAN countries (pair of correlation: R_{jt}, R_{wt})	Unconditional (local)		Unconditional (USD)	
	Mean	Std. dev	Mean	Std. dev
Singapura $\varrho(R_{STI}, R_{MSCI})$	0.325	0.215	0.316	0.224
Malaysia $\varrho(R_{KLCI}, R_{MSCI})$	0.181	0.250	0.105	0.256
Indonesia $\varrho(R_{IHSG}, R_{MSCI})$	−0.132	0.252	−0.259	0.235
Thailand $\varrho(R_{SET}, R_{MSCI})$	0.280	0.237	0.230	0.253
Philippines $\varrho(R_{PSI}, R_{MSCI})$	0.078	0.230	0.008	0.238

Source: Setyawan [14]; R_{jt}, market index return of each country; R_{wt}, return *MSCI.*

Table 1.
Unconditional correlation country level (2006–2009: weekly).

USD), Indonesia (USD), and Thailand (LOC). The comparison between standard deviations and the mean of each pair of correlations is actually identical to the Sharpe ratio formula used to measure portfolio performance [see Chen et al. [6]]. One form of practical implication is the comparison between mean and standard deviation which refers to Sharpe ratio as the benchmark for benefits of international diversification [see Piumsombun [21], Hwang and Sitorus [4], and Do et al. [5]].

4.2 Benefits of international diversification with industrial level correlations

As seen in **Table 2**, all the standard deviations for each type of correlation EW-LOC, VW-LOC, EW-USD, and VW-USD have values below the mean related to the 10 GICS industry sectors. These results confirm the argumentation that diversification between industries in ASEAN is more effective than diversification between countries and supports the study of Ratner and Leal [2], Richard [3], Hwang and Sitorus [4], and Do et al. [5] that for the 2006–2009 period, the correlation between the index returns of each ASEAN country and MSCI's high returns will lead to the more important industry effects than the country effect for global investors. But what's interesting in **Table 2** is the higher unconditional correlation of some sectors such as basic materials, financial institution, and property and real estate.

According to Kim [11] referred to by Piumsombun [21], Hwang and Sitorus [4], and Chen et al. [6], the cause of the high correlation of the three sectors is the specification of the EW-LOC, VW-LOC, EW-USD, and VW-USD, as follows:

- EW-LOC = R_{ijt} correlation (industry return i in country j at t) and R_{wt} [MSCI return (w) on t] equally weighted; local exchange rate with the formula ϱ [E (R_{ijt}) EW-LOC, R_{wt}] = Cov [E (R_{ijt}) EW-LOC, R_{wt}]/σ E (R_{ijt}) EW-LOC x σR_{wt}
- VW-LOC = R_{ijt} correlation (industry return i in country j in t) and R_{wt} [MSCI return (w) on t] in a value-weighted manner; local exchange rate with the formula ϱ [E (R_{ijt}) VW-LOC, R_{wt}] = Cov [E (R_{ijt}) VW-LOC, R_{wt}]/σ E (R_{ijt}) VW-LOC x σR_{wt}.
- EW-USD = R_{ijt} correlation (industry return i in country j to t) and R_{wt} [MSCI return (w) on t] equally weighted; USD exchange rate with the formula ϱ [E (R_{ijt}) EW-USD, R_{wt}] = Cov [E (R_{ijt}) EW-USD, R_{wt}]/σ E (R_{ijt}) EW-USD x σR_{wt}
- VW-USD = R_{ijt} correlation (industry return i in country j in t) and R_{wt} [MSCI return (w) on t] in a value-weighted manner; the USD exchange rate with the formula ϱ [E (R_{ijt}) VW-USD, R_{wt}] = Cov [E (R_{ijt}) VW-USD, R_{wt}]/σ E (R_{ijt}) VW-USD x σR_{wt}

Industry sector (GICS code)	EW-LOC		VW-LOC		EW-USD		VW-USD	
	Mean	**Std. dev**	**Mean**	**Std. dev**	**Mean**	**Std. dev**	**Mean**	**Std. dev**
Oil and gas (code 10)	0.46	0.09	0.41	0.11	0.50	0.11	0.43	0.09
Basic material (code 15)	0.57	0.06	0.56	0.03	0.61	0.08	0.58	0.03
Industrial goods (code 20)	0.54	0.05	0.57	0.04	0.54	0.06	0.59	0.05
Service goods (code 25)	0.33	0.15	0.34	0.11	0.38	0.14	0.38	0.10
Consumer goods (code 30)	0.38	0.09	0.34	0.09	0.43	0.07	0.39	0.11
Health care (code 35)	0.43	0.06	0.41	0.07	0.44	0.08	0.43	0.07
Financial institution (code 40a)	0.58	0.07	0.55	0.09	0.56	0.08	0.57	0.08
Property and real estate (code 40b)	0.52	0.04	0.49	0.09	0.57	0.06	0.55	0.06
Technology (code 45)	0.43	0.05	0.39	0.08	0.53	0.05	0.41	0.08
Utilities (code 50)	0.41	0.10	0.35	0.10	0.41	0.09	0.39	0.10

Sources: Adaption from Setyawan [14].

Table 2.
Unconditional correlation *for industry level (five ASEAN countries).*

According to Menchero and Morozov [7], market capitalization of the three sectors also contributed to the high correlation in addition to the number of industry members in GICS. Referring to **Table 2**, the practical implication is that global investors can choose the basic material industry (code 15) and industrial goods (code 20) because both have very low standard deviation values among other industries. The basis of this selection method refers to study from Hwang and Sitorus [4] and Do et al. [5], Nguyen [13], and Vo et al. [12].

4.3 Comparing benefits of international diversification (country level correlation)

Table 3 shows the results of the F-test to prove whether there are differences in the level of integration at the country level in ASEAN, which at the same time prove the presence or absence of differences in the benefits of international diversification between countries. After calculating the F-test (ANOVA), the F-calculated value of 28.643 is greater than the F-table of 2381. The F-test results showed H1 was accepted, namely, there were still differences in the level of integration in ASEAN.

The test results above support the study findings of Ratner and Leal [2], Richard [3], Hwang and Sitorus [4], and Do et al. [5] about the still relevant differences in the level of integration in ASEAN which proves the potential benefits of international diversification for global investors. Furthermore, when testing with USD currency conversion, the F-calculated value is 41.905 which is greater than the F-count when using the local currency which is 28.643.

In addition to reaffirming H1's acceptance in Section 3.2.1, it also supports the argument of Eun and Rescnick [20] that the USD value factor also plays an additional contribution to the benefits of international diversification if global investors are able to carry out a good hedging strategy, namely, entry to countries in ASEAN

Pair of correlation	Mean	Std. dev	F-test
Panel A: local currency			
STI and MSCI	0.325	0.215	28.643***
KLCI and MSCI	0.181	0.250	
IHSG and MSCI	−0.132	0.252	
SET and MSCI	0.280	0.237	
PSI and MSCI	0.078	0.230	
Panel B: USD currency			
STI and MSCI	0.316	0.224	41.905***
KLCI and MSCI	0.105	0.256	
IHSG and MSCI	-0.259	0.235	
SET and MSCI	0.230	0.253	
PSI and MSCI	0.008	0.238	

****Significant at the 1% level.*
Source: Adaptation from Setyawan [14] and Setyawan and Wibowo [15].

Table 3.
F-test for comparison of international diversification benefit at country level.

that are experiencing a strengthening (appreciation) of their local currency against the USD. Instead, this global investor will opt out of countries in ASEAN which are currently experiencing a depreciation of their local currency against the USD. This hedging pattern is recommended by Samsi [22] and Omay and Iren [23].

Returning to **Table 3**, global investors continue to target Indonesia as their portfolio target. This is because Indonesia has a negative correlation when using local currency and USD. The nature of the correlation is negative because Indonesia has the highest yields in ASEAN (see Aggarwal et al. [24]). The Malaysian stock exchange is not a global investor portfolio target because the standard deviation is higher than the mean. The results of this test support the findings of Omay and Iren [23]. Malaysia is still not a mainstay portfolio since local authorities are still so restrictive.

4.4 Comparing benefits of international diversification (industry level correlation)

The purpose of the analysis in **Tables 4** and **5** is to find out whether there are differences in the level of integration at the industry level in ASEAN. The difference in the level of integration determines the benefits of diversification between industries referring to Roll [1], Hwang and Sitorus [4], Do et al. [5], Setyawan [14], and Setyawan and Wibowo [15].

Based on the F-test results in **Table 4** panel A, it is evident that there are differences in the level of integration of the industry level in ASEAN. These results support the findings of Roll [1], Hwang and Sitorus [4], Do et al. [5], Setyawan [14], and Setyawan and Wibowo [15]. If considered in panel A, all industries have the potential benefits of diversification, referring to Chen et al. [6], namely, the value of standard deviation is smaller than that of the mean.

When analyzing the currency to the USD, H1 is still accepted, that is, there are still differences in the level of integration of the industrial level in ASEAN, with an F-count value of 1.578, significant at the 5% level. These results again support

Industry sector	Mean	Std. dev	F-test
Panel A: correlation model of EW-LOC			
Oil and gas	0.459	0.091	1.980***
Basic material	0.568	0.062	
Industrial goods	0.541	0.051	
Service goods	0.332	0.149	
Consumer goods	0.377	0.090	
Health care	0.431	0.063	
Financial institution	0.576	0.072	
Property and real estate	0.519	0.043	
Technology	0.430	0.049	
Utilities	0.414	0.101	
Panel B: correlation model of EW-USD			
Oil and gas	0.507	0.106	1.578**
Basic material	0.609	0.078	
Industrial goods	0.541	0.056	
Services goods	0.382	0.137	
Consumer goods	0.427	0.075	
Health care	0.442	0.082	
Financial institution	0.556	0.077	
Property and real estate	0.575	0.065	
Technology	0.531	0.055	
Utilities	0.412	0.089	

Source: Adaptation from Setyawan [14] and Setyawan and Wibowo [15].

Table 4.
F-test for comparison of international diversification benefit at industry level (correlation model EW).

Roll [1], Hwang and Sitorus [4], Do et al. [5], Setyawan [14], and Setyawan and Wibowo [15].

The next analysis is to change the EW proxy to VW, which includes the market capitalization factor of each industry in calculating the correlation according to Kim [11]. Based on **Table 5** panels A and B, the results of the F-test still receive H1 in Section 3.2.2, namely, F-arithmetic of 1.571 and 1.591, which is significant at the 5% level. These results reaffirm support for Roll [1], Hwang and Sitorus [4], Do et al. [5], Setyawan [14], and Setyawan and Wibowo [15], namely, the wide availability of the potential benefits of industrial diversification in ASEAN.

Referring to the study of Ratner and Leal [2] and Hwang and Sitorus [4], if a comparison of panels A and B of **Table 6** is done above, then the entire industry has a standard deviation value smaller than that of the mean. In addition, it can be seen that the industrial sector which has the biggest contribution is in industry diversification. When referring to panels A and B, the basic material industry shows the biggest contribution. This can be seen from the value of the smallest standard deviation. If it is discussed that the industrial sector is not contributing, it can be seen in panel A that is Goods Services and in panel B is Consumer Goods.

Industry sector	Mean	Std. dev	F-test
Panel A: correlation model of VW-LOC			
Oil and gas	0.412	0.107	1.571**
Basic material	0.561	0.026	
Industrial goods	0.570	0.043	
Services goods	0.338	0.113	
Consumer goods	0.340	0.096	
Health care	0.415	0.068	
Financial institution	0.553	0.087	
Property and real estate	0.487	0.089	
Technology	0.392	0.080	
Utilities	0.353	0.105	
Panel B: correlation model of VW USD			
Oil and gas	0.422	0.096	1.591**
Basic material	0.584	0.029	
Industrial goods	0.595	0.052	
Services goods	0.381	0.103	
Consumer goods	0.399	0.116	
Health care	0.428	0.073	
Financial institution	0.566	0.083	
Property and real estate	0.549	0.060	
Technology	0.418	0.083	
Utilities	0.389	0.108	

Sources: Adaptation from Setyawan [14] and Setyawan and Wibowo [15]

Table 5.
F-test for comparison of international diversification benefit at industry level (correlation model EW).

Country level correlation		Industry level correlation			
LOC	USD	EW-LOC	EW-USD	VW-LOC	VW-USD
Indonesia	Indonesia	Industrial goods	Industrial goods	Basic material	Basic material
Philippines	Philippines	Property and real estate	Property and real estate	Industrial goods	Industrial goods
Malaysia	Malaysia	Technology	Technology	Health care	Health care

Table 6.
The names of countries and industries that should be selected in this study portfolio.

Then overall I can show the practical implications, namely, which industry sector and which countries will be the mainstay portfolio in **Table 6** (sourced from **Tables 3–5** previously). The number of countries and industries in the mainstay portfolio is at least two, confirming Hwang and Sitorus [4], Do et al. [5], Nguyen [13], and also Vo et al. [12]. In **Table 6** I set three of them.

The portfolio above is arranged from top to bottom as a priority portfolio. Thus the best portfolio by country is Indonesia while for the industrial sector; we can look for industrial goods and basic material.

5. Conclusion

This study succeeded in proving the difference in the level of integration between country and industry levels in ASEAN with unconditional correlation (Pearson). In testing the differences in the level of integration at the country level, Indonesia shows the nature of negative correlations that ensure there are potential benefits of international diversification for global investors. Furthermore, in testing differences in the level of integration at the industry level by using the correlation of EW-LOC, EW-USD, VW-LOC, and VW-USD, it has been found that the potential benefits of international diversification between industries have a smaller value of standard deviation than that of the mean. Both of these test results prove the importance of correlation as a measure of capital market integration as well as international diversification.

This study also yields practical implications that by distinguishing the benefits of international diversification between countries and industries, which countries and industries can be found as a mainstay portfolio. Although this study has not succeeded in determining the name of one industry in one country. This is due to the limitations of the GICS database. Estimation only of one industry in one country is still rarely done.

Besides the limitation above, this study has the disadvantage of not using correlation for integration models such as the VAR and VECM cointegration models. Future research can use unconditional and conditional correlations as endogenous variables in the integration equation model in ASEAN with the SUR (Seemingly Unrelated Regression) technique with the data from 2012–2020. This is for capturing some structural break data that occurred, namely, the continued impact of the US subprime mortgage global financial crisis, the emergence of Bitcoin and many kinds of crypto currencies, and impacts of the US and China trade war.

Author details

Ignatius Roni Setyawan
Faculty of Economics and Business, Tarumanagara University, Jakarta, Indonesia

*Address all correspondence to: ignronis@gmail.com; ign.s@fe.untar.ac.id

References

[1] Roll R. Industrial structure and the comparative behavioral of international stock market indices. Journal of Finance. 1992;**47**(1):3-41

[2] Ratner M, Leal RPC. Sector integration and the benefits of global diversifications. Multinational Finance Journal. 2005;**9**(3/4):237-269

[3] Richard A. Big fish in small ponds: The trading behavior and price impact of foreign investors in Asian emerging equity markets. Journal of Financial and Quantitative Analysis. 2005;**40**(1):1-27

[4] Hwang P, Sitorus RE. A study of financial integration and optimal diversification strategy in ASEAN equity market. Journal of Economic Integration. 2014;**29**(3):496-519

[5] Do HQ, Bhatti MI, Konya L. On ASEAN capital market and industry integration: A review. Corporate Ownership and Control. 2016;**2**(1):8-23

[6] Chen MP, Chung DT, Lin YH. Assessing international financial integration: Do industry and firm-specific characteristic matter? Evidence from the Japanese Market. Economic Research. 2018;**31**(1):860-879

[7] Menchero J, Morozov A. The Relative Strengths of Industry and Country Factors in Global Equity Markets, *Research Insight* from MSCI BARRA (www.msci.com); 2011. pp. 1-20

[8] Endri. Integrasi Pasar Saham ASEAN dengan Menggunakan Pendekatan Structural VAR, Disertasi Program Pasca Sarjana Ilmu Manajemen FE-UI; 2010

[9] Robiyanto R, Ernayani R. Capital market integration in some ASEAN countries revisited. Jurnal Manajemen. 2018;**22**(2):205-222

[10] Click RW, Plummer MG. Stock market integration in ASEAN after the Asian financial crisis. Journal of Asian Economics. 2005;**16**(1):5-28

[11] Kim IW. Equally-weighted market return and value-weighted market return as a *Proxy* of the market indices: An empirical study. Akron Business and Economic Review. 1989;**20**(1):64-72

[12] Vo DH, Pham TN, Pham TTV, Truong LM, Nyuyen TC. Risk, return and portfolio optimization for various industries in the ASEAN region. Borsa Istanbul Review. 2019;**19**(2):132-138

[13] Nguyen TL. Diversification and bank efficiency in six ASEAN countries. Global Finance Journal. 2018;**37**:57-78

[14] Setyawan IR. Pengaruh Tingkat Kompetisi Intra Industri dan Market Openness Level terhadap Tingkat Integrasi Lima Pasar Modal di ASEAN. Disertasi Program Pasca Sarjana Ilmu Manajemen FE-UI; 2011

[15] Setyawan IR, Wibowo B. Determinant of capital market integration: The Case of ASEAN and implication to China. In: Foo CT, editor. Finance and Strategy Inside China. Springer; 2019. pp. 91-111. DOI: 10.1007/978-981-13-2841-1_8

[16] Ruefli TW. Ordinal Time-Series Analysis: Methodology and Applications in Management Strategy and Policy. London, England: Quorum Books Inc.; 1990. pp. 33-47 and 154-155

[17] Engle R. Dynamic conditional correlation: A simple class of multivariate generalized autoregressive conditional heteroscedasticity models. Journal of Business & Economic Statistics. 2002;**20**(3):339-350

[18] Luzey BM, Zhang QY. Does cultural distance matter in international stock

market comovement? Evidence from emerging economies around the world. Emerging Markets Review. 2010;**11**:62-78

[19] Dutt P, Mihov I. Stock market comovements and industrial structure. In: Working Paper in European Summer Symposium in International Macroeconomics. Tarragona, Spain; 2008. pp. 1-39

[20] Eun CS, Rescnick BG. International diversification of investment portfolios: U.S. and Japanese perspectives. Management Science. 1994;**40**(1):140-161

[21] Piumsombun K. Assessing ASEAN Capital Market Integration [thesis]. Denmark: Copenhagen Business School; 2013

[22] Samsi SM. Stock Market and Economic Growth in ASEAN-5 [Dissertation]. Faculty of Economics and Administration University of Malaya. 2017

[23] Omay T, Iren P. Behavior of foreign investors in Malaysian stock market in times of crisis: A non linear approach. Journal of Asian Economics. 2019;**60**:85-100

[24] Aggarwal S, Faircloth S, Liu C, Rhee SG. Why do foreign investors underperform domestic investors in trading activities? Evidence from Indonesia. Journal of Financial Markets. 2009;**12**:32-53

Chapter 5

Diaspora Investment to Help Achieve the SDGs in Africa: Prospects and Trends

Paul Asquith and Stella Opoku-Owusu

Abstract

Governments and the private sector have traditionally viewed the diaspora as both ongoing providers of financial capital at the micro level, and, as consumers. While recognition of the diaspora's role in 'doing development' has grown, and the diaspora are increasingly seen as important development stakeholders, they are still not viewed as significant social investors by governments, the private sector, or indeed the diaspora themselves. This represents a missed opportunity for harnessing and seeking to scale up diaspora investments for socio-economic growth, especially given the gap in financing available to deliver the Sustainable Development Goals (SDGs). This chapter offers an overview of diaspora investment types and forms, dividing these into four main types, namely: diaspora philanthropy, diaspora remittances, diaspora direct investment (DDI), and diaspora Portfolio Investment (DPI). It argues that governments, financial institutions, the private sector, and the diaspora themselves should view diaspora investments as part of the development financing mix, especially as part of 'blended finance' packages.

Keywords: diaspora investment, development finance, Sustainable Development Goals (SDGs), affordable housing in Africa

1. Introduction

This chapter examines trends in diaspora investment, and in particular how such investments can drive socio-economic growth and development in countries of origin, as well as in countries of transit and destination. It argues that the African diaspora, in addition to being recognised as the source of significant resource flows to countries of origin or heritage through remittances, should also be seen—and be encouraged to see themselves—as significant social investors in African development in their own right. This in turn creates potential opportunities for governments, financial institutions, and the private sector to harness and scale up these investments for economic growth, especially in Africa's emerging and frontier markets, by developing and deploying a combination of policy frameworks and investment vehicles targeting diaspora investors.

This is even more critical in supporting the implementation of the SDGs on the continent. The projected shortfall in development financing needed to achieve the Sustainable Development Goals globally, is estimated at around $30 bn USD per annum. This means that innovative approaches to development financing are required more now than ever before. The Addis Ababa Action Agenda on financing the SDGs, agreed in 2015, is explicit that governments, civil society, and the private sector will all have to contribute more resources to achieve these goals.

At the same time, developing countries are seeking to raise investment finance to meet growing infrastructure, energy, and other needs in national development planning. The challenges to doing so in frontier and emerging economies are all the greater given current market and investment trends. There is a lot of innovation in diaspora interventions with potential for significant results. This chapter argues that more focus on diaspora investors and diaspora investment could yield significant results for Africa's emerging markets and for helping achieve the SDGs.

2. Methodology

The research methodology involved extensive review and analysis of corporate, financial, legal, institutional, and academic literature. This included African financial institutions, innovative finance schemes, and social enterprise structures. Research consultation questions were used to guide face-to-face and telephone interviews and discussions with practitioners, policymakers, and potential diaspora investors in Europe and Africa. The review was also informed by internal AFFORD reports and data, drawing on its experience of delivering diaspora enterprise and finance initiatives in Africa over the last decade.

People consulted included officials of the African Union and the World Bank. Participation in forums such as the Global Forum on Migration and Development (GFMD) in Marrakech in December 2018 enabled consultations with development and investment policymakers and practitioners from government, multilateral, diaspora, media, money transfer, and other organisations.

3. Defining diaspora investors and investments

A range of definitions have been proposed for the term diaspora, and for what constitutes diaspora investment. Definitions of diaspora can vary and may also be contested by some groups. However, for the purposes of this chapter, the African Union (AU) definition is used whereby:

> *'the African Diaspora consists of peoples of African origin living outside the continent, irrespective of their citizenship and nationality and who are willing to contribute to the development of the continent and the building of the African Union' [1]*

According to Plaza and Ratha, the size of the African diaspora totalled over 30.6 million in 2011 [2]. However, this number is a significant underestimate as it only counts the total foreign-born population and therefore excludes second-, third-, and subsequent-generation migrants who in many cases maintain ties to their country of origin and/or heritage. It also excludes the millions from the historic Atlantic Diaspora, which the AU includes in its definition of the diaspora and as part of its concept of a sixth region.

As Oviatt and McDougall argue, due to the sentimental attachment to their countries of origin, diaspora transnationalism initiates investments; connects home and host countries in political, economic, and social issues; creates jobs; and provides business, technical, and technological information about host countries to their country of origin [3]. Moreover, such investments need not be necessarily for financial return but also for socio-economic improvement and feelings of duty and obligation to their country of origin [2].

Diaspora investors are more likely to invest in their country of origin than non-diaspora investors as they are privy to a more sophisticated understanding of the governance and business in-country, and may therefore have a differing understanding of risk from other investors. Plaza and Ratha characterise this as diaspora investors taking advantage of information asymmetries, and suggest this is an area where diaspora investments should be encouraged so as to take advantage of their comparative advantage in this regard [2].

4. Types of diaspora investments

Faal [4] provides a detailed breakdown of diaspora investment types and forms, dividing these into four main types, namely: diaspora philanthropy, diaspora remittances, diaspora direct investment (DDI), and Diaspora Portfolio Investment (DPI), mirroring the established distinctions between FDI and FPI [4]. Although the former of these, diaspora philanthropy, is an important form of financial contribution to development, it falls out of the scope of this chapter as it does not fit the strict definition of financial investment in that no profit or financial return is expected or received by the diaspora or migrants or who make such contributions [5, 6].[1] There are some rare exceptions to this though, such as Rwanda's Agaciro Fund [5], which has relied on philanthropic donations from the diaspora, and is being developed as a sovereign wealth fund with a strong investment element.

4.1 Diaspora remittances

Diaspora remittances have been the subject of numerous studies at the macro and micro levels, and there is strong evidence that remittances are a major engine for development in Africa. According to the World Bank in 2019, formal remittances to Africa reached $86 bn USD [7]. Of this, 70% was received by Egypt, Nigeria, and Morocco. In the case of Nigeria, the amount remitted in 2018 ($22 bn USD) was larger than the entire federal budget that year ($18 bn USD). For five countries, formal remittances alone account for over 10% of GDP, namely, Comoros, The Gambia, Lesotho, Cape Verde, and Liberia. In addition to formal channels, migrants and the diaspora still use unregistered and informal channels to send money to Africa. They also send in-kind remittances. If funds sent through formal, informal, and in-kind remittances are taken into account, it is estimated that annual remittances to Africa can be as high as $200 bn USD [8].[2]

The World Bank notes that remittance transaction costs for Africa are the highest in the world at 9% as compared to the global average cost of 7%. Remittance costs within Africa are particularly high, the highest costs being transactions

---

[1] Faal ([4], pp. 22–37) notes that he main forms of diaspora philanthropy are: Direct donations to civil society, religious, social and community appeals and schemes; Collective remittances channelled through Home Town, Community and Alumni Associations (HCA) and diaspora networks; and national Trust Funds such as the Rwanda Agaciro Development Fund (ADF) set up in 2012, which had an asset value of about USD43m in 2016, and the Ethiopia Diaspora Trust Fund (EDTF) which was set up in August 2018 and had raised about USD4m from 20,000 people in 70 countries by April 2019.

[2] The Lead Economist on Migration and Remittances at the World Bank, Dilip Ratha [8], has stated that "unrecorded flows through informal channels are believed to be at least 50% larger than recorded flows." The SSRC reported that informal remittances are estimated to vary from 35% to 250% of formal flows [9].

originating from South Africa, as high as 18%. The two cheapest intra-African remittance corridors were about 3.5%, these being Senegal-Mali and Cote D'Ivoire-Mali. The cheapest international corridors were about 4%, being France-Cameroon and France-Comoros. It should be noted that SDG Target 10.7 (10.C) states: 'By 2030, reduce to less than 3 per cent the transaction costs of migrant remittances and eliminate remittance corridors with costs higher than 5 per cent' [10].

Formal remittances to Africa, which keep growing, are higher than all other forms of non-trade financial flows, as shown in **Table 1** below:

Inflows to Africa ($ Billion USD)	2011	2012	2013	2014	2015
Migrant and diaspora remittances	59.6	64.3	63.7	67.2	64.8
Foreign direct investment (FDI)	49.8	49.4	53.1	56.0	51.3
Official development assistance	51.6	51.8	56.8	54.3	51.0
Foreign portfolio investment (FPI)	21.6	34.3	23.0	21.3	15.7

Source: UNCTAD [11].

Table 1.
Financial inflows to Africa in 2011–2015.

The World Bank has identified a number of factors that increase the propensity for remittance receivers to invest:

- 'Remittance flows are viewed by the household as transitory rather than permanent and thus should be saved (and invested) rather than spent.

- The sender conditions the remittance on it being spent for particular purposes, which are more likely to involve investment than current consumption. Examples include education or the purchase of new farm machinery.

- The remittance is targeted (or "tagged") to household members more likely to use the funds for investment purposes (women rather than men).

- Households practice a form of mental accounting with their overall budget, with remittances being disproportionately put in accounts set aside for investment purposes'.

- Remittances also have the effect of increasing the likelihood of entrepreneurial enterprises for middle-income households [2].

4.2 Diaspora Direct Investment (DDI)

This relates to direct investments whereby the investor has origins or heritage in the foreign country of investment, irrespective of their nationality. The notion of heritage-based African DDI is practically useful because millions of African diasporans are unable to definitely pinpoint their origins to a particular country in Africa. However, unlike FDI flows, which are officially monitored by a range of multilateral institutions, there is a dearth of reliable data on formal DDI flows to Africa, and it is recommended that annual surveys should aim to gather data on levels of DDI to inform investment trends and also policy-making in this area.

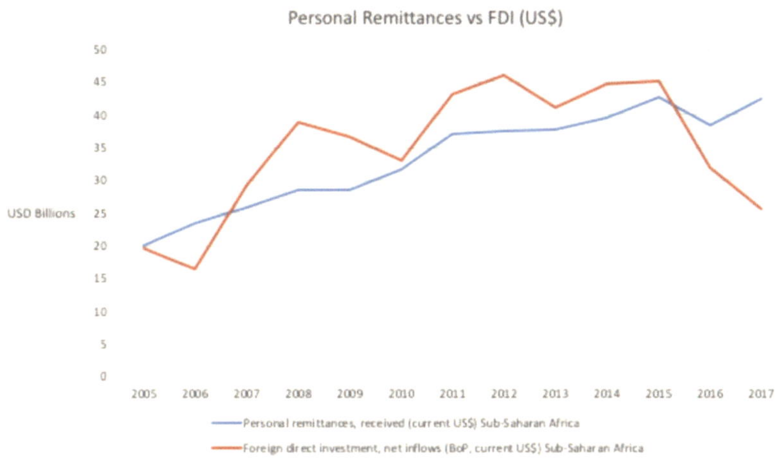

Figure 1.
Remittances vs. FDI. Source: World Bank [12].

The relationship between DDI and diaspora remittances is a complex one, in part due to the fact that DDI (like remittances) includes both formal and informal channels. There is significant evidence that remittances are counter-cyclical, inasmuch as remittance flows tend to increase in times of crisis or conflict, when non-diaspora investors may be looking to exit difficult markets. Certainly, remittances tend to be far less volatile than other inflows such as FDI as **Figure 1** demonstrates.

As the African Development Bank [13] notes, 'remittances, over the years, were observed to be more stable than other capital inflows. Moreover, both Newland and Patrick (2004) and Africa Development Bank (2012) underscore that household remittances, if significant and supported by appropriate policies and enabling conducive environment, can generate multiplier effects, which may provide the basis for more sustainable poverty reduction' [14]. It is not yet clear however if diaspora investments beyond remittances display the same tendencies, and there is a need for further research and data on this subject.

Informal DDI, like informal remittances, include investments to unincorporated businesses. In Africa, the informal sector forms a significant percentage of the economy, providing up to 65% of all jobs, and it is estimated that investments in the informal sector make up a significant component of diaspora investment activity, often investing in family MSMEs [15]. Moreover, a proportion of remittances are used for formal and informal investments, typically in the MSME and property sectors. According to the World Bank, 20% of all monies remitted are used for such investment purposes; IFAD [16] uses a higher figure, noting that up to 30% of remittances are used for investment purposes, typically in the informal sector [17]. Faal [4] also notes that DDI is 'a vital and significant source of capital in the sector of the self-employed, sole traders, partnerships, unregistered trade agents, occasional and accidental entrepreneurs. Similar to remittances, individual DDIs may be small, but the aggregate is likely to be very high' [4].[3]

Another form of DDI that should be considered is in-kind DDI. While FDI may be used to procure key assets such as machinery or business equipment, DDI is more likely to include in-kind provision both of physical assets and also technical and management skills and experience. Indeed, as Ardovino and Debass argue,

[3] Ref. [4], p. 30.

DDI provides a package that can include both capital investment and technological development ('brain gain') [18]. In addition, DDI can operate as a business catalyst in countries of residence and/or transit, and helps facilitate bilateral trade and development links [18].

Diaspora members already make great use of collective remittances such as those generated by hometown and alumni associations, both for philanthropy, and also for small-scale impact investments in the African social economy; some of this activity therefore extends beyond the philanthropic into definitions of DDI. Moreover, the diaspora pool funds through diaspora investment clubs and business angel networks, which are used to make direct investments in diverse businesses, as well as investments in regulated financial products [19].[4] However, the data on the value of DDI from different sources are often lacking and there is scope for multilateral institutions monitoring DDI and FDI to improve measurement of this sort of activity.

4.3 Diaspora real estate as DDI

Acquisition and development of real estate is often the biggest investment that individuals in the diaspora make in their countries of origin or heritage. Diaspora investors may seek to acquire real estate for multiple reasons, ranging from retirement accommodation, use by extended family to rental of residential or commercial units, longer term leasing or outright sale. Furthermore, the diaspora can use such assets as leverage and guarantee for local bank loans to invest in other real estate ventures and in other businesses. However, access to credit for property and real estate can be limited, both in countries of residence and in particular in countries of origin and/or heritage, and there is a potential untapped market for greater provision of mortgages in several African countries [20].[5]

While there is a debate over the extent to which diaspora real estate can be considered DDI, centring on how such investments are productive, it is clear that much (if not most) of such activity can be classed as such. Indeed, the World Bank has previously undertaken household surveys to estimate the value of remittances spent on real estate that can inform methodologies for assessing levels of real estate DDI in Africa [17].

4.4 Diaspora portfolio investments (DPIs)

FDI is typically contrasted with Foreign Portfolio Investments (FPIs), defined as 'cross border transactions and positions involving debt or equity securities, other than those included in direct investment or reserve assets' [21]. Securities are negotiable and tradable financial instruments representing an ownership position in an asset, be it company stocks and shares, corporate or sovereign bonds or debenture, derivative contracts, or other forms of shareholding or debt.

In comparison to other parts of the world, FPI in Africa is small and relatively underdeveloped. In 2017, the value of global FPI assets was 60 tn $USD [19]. There are no directly comparable data for Africa, but the value of outstanding African

[4] See inter alia. African Diaspora Network's African Diaspora Symposium https://www.adis2019.com/; Diaspora Investment Club https://diasporainvestmentclub.com/investing-2/investing-in-africa/; Club Efficience https://club-efficience.com/en/efficience-africa-fund-en/; African Business Angel Network https://abanangels.org/the-aban-network/; AFFORD Business Club https://afford-uk.org/what-we-do/projects/abc-2/

[5] Ref. [4], p. 30.

Eurobonds in the same period was USD92 Billion [20]. This indicates that African FPI assets are a fraction of a percent of global assets.

Similarly, diaspora investors also invest in what may be termed 'Diaspora Portfolio Investment' (DPI). Terrazas defines DPI as: 'Investments made in the country of origin by a diasporan or groups of diasporans, including (1) the purchase of sovereign bonds issued by the country of origin government, (2) the purchase of equity in companies in the country of origin, (3) investments made in fixed-income or other securities that lend money to firms exclusively in the country of origin, (4) stock purchases in the country of origin, and (5) investments made in mutual funds comprised of firms in the country of origin' [22].

Unlike direct investment, ownership of securities does not generally lead to involvement in the management of the enterprise, venture, or asset. It is a form of passive investment, which is one of the reasons why the sector is regulated by public authorities to, among other things, protect investors. In this respect portfolio investment products may be more suitable and less risky for diaspora investors.

In the specific case of the African diaspora, DPI also includes portfolio investments made by multigenerational diaspora investors in their country of heritage (rather than just country of birth or parental origin), irrespective of their current nationality. African DPI thus includes investments by African Americans, Afro-Brazilians and other members of the historic Atlantic Diaspora who may not even be able to pinpoint their origins to a particular country in Africa. Diaspora bonds and Diaspora Mutual Funds are therefore important emergent DPI products targeting diaspora investment appetites.

Neither the World Bank, nor IMF or any other global or regional Multilateral Financial Institution measure and monitor Diaspora Portfolio Investment (DPI) in a structured, standardised, and regular manner. A better understanding of this could provide an opportunity for governments, private sector, and the diaspora to support SDG financing gaps by maximising the contributions and benefits of DPI for social investment purposes.

5. Examples of DDI and DPI programmes

5.1 DDI programmes

Several African countries have schemes backed by policy and legislation that offer DDI incentives and tax breaks comparable to those available for FDI. Some countries provide grants, co-finance, and loan guarantees to diaspora investors. For some countries like Gambia and Ghana, the incentive programme is managed by the national inward investment promotion agency and is a variant of the FDI programme [23].[6] Typically, such schemes tend to set a lower threshold of cash investment requirement for diaspora investors to access to incentives.

Some countries set up additional specialist diaspora co-finance and Diaspora Development Funds to stimulate DDI. For Morocco, the 'MDM Invest' programme enables Moroccans Living Abroad to access a grant of up to 5 Million Dirham (over $500,000 USD) or 10% of costs, for projects implemented in Morocco [24]. For Senegal, the 'FAISE' programme provides low-interest, 5-year loans of up to 15 Million CFA (over $25,000 USD), with repayment holidays, for diaspora projects

[6] See, inter alia, Gambia: http://giepa.gm/Investment%20and%20Export%20Incentives%20and%20Support%20to%20MSMEs; Ghana: https://www.gipcghana.com/invest-in-ghana/why-ghana/tax-regime-and-incentives.html.

[25]. Other countries have made it easy for the diaspora to access domestic investment incentives such as loan guarantee schemes.

In addition to state-led DDI incentives, there are a number of diaspora co-financing programmes operating from Europe and North America. These include: 'Diaspora Programme Support' social enterprise grants of $75,000 USD (Denmark); 'African Diaspora Marketplace' business plan competition prizes of USD70,000 (USA); 'AFFORD Business Centre (ABC)' social enterprise co-finance of $38,000 uSD; 'PRA/OSIM' enterprise and project co-finance of $34,000 USD (France); 'Entrepreneurship by Diaspora for Development' technical support (Netherlands); 'MeetAfrica' providing technical assistance for the establishment of diaspora enterprises in Africa (France and Germany) [26].[7] A structured DDI measurement methodology therefore needs to map and monitor output from the various diaspora incentive schemes across Africa.

5.2 DPI programmes: diaspora bonds and mutual funds

Diaspora bonds are perhaps the best-known example of DPI programmes. Israel bonds have been issued since 1951, raising approximately $40bn USD by 2015 to finance a range of infrastructure, security and strategic developments [27]. India issued the $1.6 bn USD Indian Development Bonds (IDB) in 1991 to address balance of payments crisis; the $4.2 bn USD Resurgent India Bonds (RIB) in 1998 in response to economic sanctions imposed after nuclear testing; and the $5.5bn USD India Millennium Deposits (IMD) in 2000 to capitalise on this new source of development finance [23].

African countries have successful experience of launching bonds, as examples across the continent demonstrate, but such bonds have typically been open to all investors, including foreign individuals and institutions. Despite the great potential of diaspora bonds in African markets, only four African countries have ever issued bonds packaged and targeted specifically for the African diaspora. Of the diaspora bonds issued by Ghana, Ethiopia, Kenya, and Nigeria, only the 2014 Bank of Kenya Infrastructure Bond and the 2017 Nigeria Diaspora Bond were fully subscribed [28, 29]. Nevertheless, there is an increasing appetite to develop investment products that can tap into diaspora investments and savings. AFFORD is currently developing a pilot commercial bond in partnership with the e Rwandan Ministry of Finance and Economic Planning that is aimed at financing affordable housing for key workers in Kigali.

Diaspora mutual funds are a distinct form of DPI where investors are exclusively diaspora and friends of the diaspora. These are structured to meet the interests and needs of the diaspora and marketing activities are targeted at existing and new diaspora investors. Continental banks such as Ecobank and national and regional banks like KCB offer mutual fund products to their clients who hold distinctive diaspora bank accounts [30]. As with diaspora bonds, however, there are limited bespoke Diaspora mutual funds available in the African financial marketplace. The literature makes reference to schemes such as the Liberian Diaspora Social Investment Fund, Zambia First Investment Fund, and Rwanda Diaspora mutual fund (RDMF), but these have yet to take off at scale [26].

[7] See, inter alia: Denmark: https://drc.ngo/media/1893463/new-infographics_4-parts-in-one-file.pdf; USA: http://diaspora.globalinnovationexchange.org/organizations/african-diaspora-marketplace; United Kingdom: http://www.afford-diasporafinance.org/; France: https://www.forim.net/contenu/praosim-0; Netherlands: https://www.connectingdiaspora.org/ed4d/call-for-business-ideas/; France & Germany: https://www.campusfrance.org/en/MEETAfrica-creation-entreprises

6. Harnessing diaspora investment trends

The range of sectors and trends of African diaspora investors are broad, even if a lot of their investment activity is channelled through the informal and MSME sectors through family networks. Nevertheless the impact of this activity extends beyond this to fund expansion of diaspora-based businesses and greenfield ventures; technology, professional and skill-based consultancies and enterprise, and real estate, heritage, tourism, and export sector businesses [4]. Diaspora investments tend to fund services and light industry, rather than manufacturing and heavy industry, and can include in-kind input such as technical skills and plant, machinery, and equipment. Collective remittances are used for diverse ventures and projects, and are channelled to cooperatives, and social and community enterprises.

A range of barriers to diaspora investment have been identified by surveys such as those conducted by UNCTAD [11] and Commonwealth Foundation [31]. These include: a lack of knowledge of the country of investment (particularly among 2nd and 3rd generation migrants); fears of corruption, perceived political instability; fears of bureaucracy; a lack of partners in the country of origin.

Due to such factors, diaspora investment patterns often appear to be conservative (albeit far from risk averse) and mostly channelled via DDI to the informal and MSME sectors through extended family and social networks, rather than towards structured DPI products. However, remittances are an inefficient way of investing capital—the transfer costs to sub-Saharan Africa alone are on average 8.9–9.4% and the return on investment can be low.

The challenge for financial institutions, policymakers, and the private sector alike is to develop DPI products (and suitable policy and business environments) that are sufficiently attractive to encourage diaspora investors to shift away from remittances. This represents a large potential market for suitable DPI products, with a suitable range of entry points and risk profiles for different diaspora investor profiles. Trust in the institutions issuing such products is key to this, as is understanding the size, location, environment, and investor appetites of the diaspora communities concerned [32].

7. Conclusion

In this we chapter we have shown how the diaspora continues to act as an important stakeholder in economic growth and development in countries of origin and/or transit, both through remittances but also investment in family businesses and property. Moreover, such financial contributions are mostly channelled to the informal and MSME sectors, which in Africa are the motor of economic growth and, critically, job creation.

The scale and extent of diaspora investments in countries of origin and/or heritage is vast, far outstripping bilateral ODA and indeed FDI in many African countries. Diaspora communities therefore represent increasingly important economic (as well as political) constituencies for governments in countries of origin. As noted above, diaspora investments can help countries overcome the development financing gap and raise additional investment finance to meet growing infrastructure, energy, and other needs in national development planning

Governments and the private sector have traditionally viewed the diaspora as both ongoing providers of financial capital at the micro level, and, as consumers. While recognition of the diaspora's role in 'doing development' has grown, and the diaspora are increasingly seen as important development stakeholders, they are still not viewed as significant social investors by governments, the private sector, or indeed the diaspora themselves. This represents a missed opportunity for harnessing and seeking to scale up diaspora investments for socio-economic growth.

This chapter argues that governments, financial institutions, the private sector, and the diaspora should view diaspora investments as part of the development financing mix, especially as part of 'blended finance' packages.

There are a number of ways in which this might be achieved. Firstly, financial institutions and the private sector could continue to develop and market innovative financial products, especially via the use of online platforms, business incubators and accelerators, targeting the diaspora as social investors; examples include diaspora bonds.

Secondly, they could also facilitate the establishing of bank accounts, foreign currency deposit accounts, fixed-term super FX accounts, or allow diaspora the option of holding funds in either foreign currency or domestic currency with greater benefits for domestic currency.

Governments and multilateral financial institutions can develop programmes to encourage diaspora investments, in particular as part of blended finance packages, but also including the use of online platforms, business incubators and accelerators, targeting the diaspora as social investors. For such programmes to be effective, they should also include elements of match funding for diaspora investors who are exploring DDI as part of their businesses.

Remittance transfer costs to Africa remain high, and there is global consensus (as evinced by SDG target 10.c to reduce transfer fees to 3% or less) that governments, multilateral financial institutions, and the private sector should intensify efforts to reduce remittance transfer costs, to meet this SDG target. This action would return millions to senders and recipients, which can be targeted to investment purposes.

There is also a need for governments and multilateral financial institutions to develop methodologies for better monitoring of DDI and DPI flows, including publication of a DDI index. AFFORD is currently developing a more granular methodology of the 2nd edition of an African DDI Index to track diaspora investment trends in the continent and this series will be developed and extended over 2020.

Acknowledgements

The authors would like to thank Subodh Tailor at the University of Edinburgh for his help and support in compiling data for this article.

Conflict of interest

The authors declare no conflict of interest.

Author details

Paul Asquith and Stella Opoku-Owusu
African Foundation for Development (AFFORD UK), London, United Kingdom

*Address all correspondence to: paul@afford-uk.org

References

[1] Sandton Declaration: African Union. 2012. Available from: https://www.gov.za/declaration-global-african-diaspora-summit-sandton-johannesburg-south-africa

[2] Sonia P, Dilip R. Diaspora for Development in Africa (English). Washington, DC: World Bank; 2011. Available from: http://documents.worldbank.org/curated/en/389011468191676942/Diaspora-for-development-in-Africa

[3] Oviatt B, McDougall P. Defining international entrepreneurship and modeling the speed of internationalization. Entrepreneurship Theory and Practice. 2005;**29**(5):537-553

[4] Faal G. Strategic, Business and Operational Framework for an African Diaspora Finance Corporation: African Union Legacy Project on Diaspora Investment, Innovative Finance and Social Enterprise in Africa. GK Partners/African Union Commission; 2019. An abridged version is available from: https://au.int/sites/default/files/documents/37383-doc-adfc_business_framework_-_abridged_version.pdf

[5] International Forum of Sovereign Wealth Funds: Agaciro [Internet]. 2020. Available from: https://www.ifswf.org/members/rwanda

[6] Agaciro Fund [Internet]. 2011. Available from: http://www.agaciro.rw/

[7] World Bank, Migration and Remittances: Recent Developments and Outlook, Migration and Development Brief 31: April 2019. 2019. Available from: https://www.knomad.org/sites/default/files/2019-04/Migrationanddevelopmentbrief31.pdf

[8] Dilip R. Remittances: Funds for the Folks Back Home [Internet]. 2020. Available from: https://www.imf.org/external/pubs/ft/fandd/basics/remitt.htm

[9] SSRC. Topic 4: Formal vs. Informal Remittances. New York: Social Science Research Council; 2009. Available from: https://www.ssrc.org/publications/view/4297524A-B74F-DE11-AFAC-001CC477EC70/

[10] Sustainable Development Goals: Goal 10: Reduce inequality within and among countries. [Internet]. 2015. Available from: https://www.un.org/sustainabledevelopment/inequality/

[11] UNCTAD. World Investment Report 2018: Investment and New Industrial Policies. Geneva: United Nations Conference on Trade and Development (UNCTAD); 2018

[12] World Bank. Migration and Remittances: Recent Developments and Outlook. Migration and Development Brief 31: April 2019. 2019. Available from: https://www.knomad.org/sites/default/files/2019-04/Migrationanddevelopmentbrief31.pdf

[13] AfDB. Diaspora Bonds: Some Lessons for African Countries, Africa Economic Brief 3 (13). African Development Bank: Abidjan; 2012

[14] Mugano G. Diaspora investment and African national economies: Case studies. In: Hack-Polay S, editor. African Diaspora Direct Investment: Establishing the Economic and Socio-Cultural Rationale. London: Palgrave; 2018

[15] Leandro M, Andrew J, Mehmet C. The informal economy in Sub-Saharan Africa: Size and determinants. In: IMF Working Paper WP/17/156. Washington, DC: International Monetary Fund; 2017

[16] IFAD. The use of remittances and financial inclusion. 2015. Available from: https://www.ifad.org/documents/38714170/40187309/gpfi.pdf/58ce7a06-7ec0-42e8-82dc-c069227edb79

[17] Plaza S, Navarrete M, Ratha D. Migration and Remittances Household Surveys in Sub Saharan Africa: Methodological Aspects and Main Findings. Washington, DC: World Bank and African Development Bank; 2011. Available from: http://pubdocs.worldbank.org/en/866251444753456291/Plaza-Navarrete-Ratha-MethodologicalPaper.pdf

[18] Ardovino M, Debass T. Diaspora Direct Investment (DDI): The Untapped Resource for Development. Washington, DC: United States Agency for International Development (USAID); 2009

[19] IMF Coordinated Portfolio Investment Survey (CPIS). [Internet]. 2020. Available from: http://data.imf.org/?sk=B981B4E3-4E58-467E-9B90-9DE0C3367363

[20] African Eurobonds: what to look for in 2019. Business Telegraph. Jan 2019. Available from: https://thebusinesstelegraph.com/2019/01/23/african-eurobonds-what-to-look-for-in-2019

[21] IMF. Balance of Payments and International Investment Position Manual (BPM6), Chapter 6. 2007. Available from: https://www.imf.org/external/pubs/ft/bop/2007/pdf/chap6.pdf

[22] Terrazas A. Diaspora Investment in Developing and Emerging Country Capital Markets: Patterns and Prospects. Washington, DC: Migration Policy Institute; 2010

[23] Ketkar S, Ratha D. Diaspora bonds: Tapping the diaspora during difficult times. Journal of International Commerce, Economics and Policy. 2010;**1**(2):251-263. Available from: http://www.dilipratha.com/index_files/DiasporaBonds-JICEP.pdf

[24] Morocco: MDM Invest. Available from: http://www.ccg.ma/en/votre-projet/mdm-invest

[25] Senegal: Fonds d'Appui à l'Investissement des Sénégalais de l'Exterieur ['Support fund for Senegalese diaspora investment). Available from: http://faise.sn/

[26] Central Bank approves 'Diaspora Mutual Fund". New Times. [Internet]. December 2019. Available from: https://www.newtimes.co.rw/section/read/14617

[27] DCI/Israel Bonds. [Internet]. 2020. Available from: https://israelbonds.com/About-Us/DCI-Israel-Bonds.aspx

[28] Enders Mira, Development Finance: Untapped Potential [Internet]. March 2020. Available from: https://www.dandc.eu/en/article/diaspora-bonds-could-play-bigger-role-development-finance

[29] World Bank. A Billion Dollar Idea: Leveraging Migration for Financing Development. Washington, DC: World Bank; 2013. Available from: http://blogs.worldbank.org/peoplemove/files/special_topic.pdf

[30] Available from: https://ecobank.com/ng/personal-banking/everyday-banking/savings-accounts/diaspora; https://ke.kcbgroup.com/diaspora/

[31] Commonwealth Foundation. Financing the SDGs with. Diaspora Investment: Geneva. 2017;**2018**. Available from: http://thecommonwealth.org/sites/default/files/inline/2017_CW_FinancingtheSDGswithDiasporaInvestment_REPORT.PDF

[32] Commonwealth Foundation. Understanding the Investment Potential of the Commonwealth Diaspora: Results of the Commonwealth Diaspora Investor Survey. 2018. Available from: https://thecommonwealth.org/sites/default/files/inline/Understanding%20the%20Investment%20Potential%20of%20the%20Commonwealth%20Diaspora.pdf

Chapter 6

Applying Consistency Fuzzy Preference Relations to Select a Strategy that Attracts Foreign Direct Investment (FDI) in Developing Supporting Industries for Vietnam

Nguyen Xuan Huynh and Hoang Dinh Phi

Abstract

The Vietnamese government has been focused on promoting supporting industries, which may provide a "key" solution for sustained development and thereby improve the national welfare. Coincidentally, Vietnam is also focused on an optimal strategy to attract foreign direct investment (FDI that develops a strategy for supporting industries). However, these results have not been achieved due to the weaknesses of low FDI flow, the limited number of capital projects, and the inclusion of smaller enterprises with lower technology into the mix. This negative situation begs the question as to what might be the best strategy for attracting FDI that developmentally supports the Vietnamese industry. As an intended remedy, this inquiry establishes an analytical, hierarchy framework beneficial to the Vietnamese government on a best strategic method for attracting FDI to develop supporting local industries. This study utilizes fuzzy preference relations to improve the decision-making process to be both consistent and effective. The analytical results demonstrate that institutional policies, domestic supply capacity, human resources, and technological development, coupled with innovation, are the key criteria to be considered when selecting a strategy that attracts regular FDI. Furthermore, analytical results presented in this work demonstrate that the best strategies for attracting FDI to Vietnam are those that motivate sustainable economic growth on an ongoing basis.

Keywords: attracting FDI, developing supporting industries, fuzzy preference relations, multi-criteria decision-making

1. Introduction

Vietnam's supporting industries are still less developed and less competitive than those of other Asian countries, comparatively speaking [1]. Some of the major factors leading to the weakness of supporting industries in Vietnam are a distinct lack of capital, technological innovation, and management skills suitable for development purposes [2]. FDI increases economic growth of recipient countries by bringing physical change through the introduction of infrastructure, advanced technology, and management expertise [3]. It is also considered to increase domestic capital, create employment, raise personal incomes, promote technology, and generate the transfer of skills through foreign technology and know-how to boost host country economies; so, such investment is seen as the engine of economic growth in the long term [4]. Moreover, FDI is an important vehicle for the transfer of technology, as it contributes relatively more to overall growth than what domestic investment may accomplish [5]. Therefore, attracting FDI for developing supporting industries is seen to be the best strategy to solve the problem of much-needed capital obtainment.

In addition, Vietnam is still considered to be a developing country. The Vietnamese government has concentrated on attracting FDI to develop supporting industries which will add to further overall development throughout the nation as a whole [6, 7]. However, the FDI attraction necessary to develop supporting industries in Vietnam is still viewed as an inherent weakness due to low FDI inflows, the noticeably limited number of infrastructure projects, and the proliferation of smaller, lower-technology enterprises that do not significantly contribute to any great extent [6]. Moreover, the General Statistics Office (GSO) of Vietnam [8] states that the total cumulative FDI for developing supporting industries is approximately US $29.16 billion, accounting for a 46.19% of all FDI projects, and 72.25% of the total FDI value in industries, wherein 15.63% quantity of FDI projects and 16.87% of the total FDI value are shown in supporting industries. Therefore, this study demonstrates the key factors that will have the most important impact to attract FDI to develop supporting industries in Vietnam.

This study concentrates on selecting a workable strategy for attracting FDI to develop supporting industries in Vietnam. Moreover, it should be noted that FDI firms consistently perform better than domestic ones in order to drive the development of Vietnam's supporting industries [2]. It utilizes a theoretical study, and it examines the current situation of developing supporting industries coupled with the reality of attracting FDI to Vietnam. This examination is to be taken together with the results which are concomitant with interviews of government staff and policy-makers, economists, foreign investors, and managers from six supporting industries. The results have indicated that there are eight main criteria that influence the attraction of FDI to develop supporting industries [6]; and, there are three alternative strategies applicable to attracting FDI. The eight main criteria are as follows: (1) institutions and policies; (2) human resources (e.g., quantity, salary, education, skill, and morale); (3) infrastructure facilities (e.g., transport, power, information, communication, etc.); (4) domestic supply capability (total value and partition domestic supply chain and the quantity and size of supporting industries firms); (5) market size of supporting industries (i.e., the total consumption of supporting industries products); (6) technological development and innovation; (7) international cooperation and competition; and (8) other criteria (such as environmental policy, culture, tax policy, land support, corruption, etc.). When taken together, there exist various alternative strategy policies for attracting FDI to develop supporting industries, namely: (i) attracting FDI for developing supporting industries, which motivates the economy's sustainable growth; (ii) attracting FDI for developing supporting industries, which increases national competitiveness; and (iii) attracting FDI for developing supporting industries, which stimulates overall national technological development. Based on the results obtained, an analytical, hierarchy framework has been developed to assist the Vietnamese government and involved policy-makers to evaluate the practical influence of those criteria under review and to choose a strategy platform which may attract future FDI to develop supporting industries by using the established eight main criteria and three alternatives posited in this study.

This study uses AHP methodology to perform complicated pairwise comparisons among the criteria at hand. It may take considerable time to obtain a convincing consistency index with such an increasing number of criteria. From that, or because of that, the study uses the consistency fuzzy preference relations (CFPR) model [6, 9–16] useful to calculate the nature of the criteria and the adjacent alternative weighting. These results are utilized to determine the most important criteria and to select the best strategy for attracting FDI.

2. Related literature

2.1 Concepts of supporting industry and developing supporting industries in Vietnam

The term "supporting industries" is derived from Japanese literature in the mid-1980s [2, 17, 18]. It first appeared in a White Paper on Economic Cooperation of the Ministry of International Trade and Industry (MITI) of Japan [19] for the promotion of industrialization as a process and as part of directing the development of small and medium enterprises (SMEs) which were part of the Association of Southeast Asian Nations (ASEAN) country structure, especially in Singapore, Malaysia, Thailand, Indonesia, and the Philippines. The term was officially defined to signify industries that supply raw materials, parts, and capital goods for assembly-type industries. Currently, the term "supporting industries" is widely used, especially in East Asia. It is interpreted differently in different fields of activities [2, 18, 20]. In Vietnam, the use of supporting industries is defined in accordance with Decision No. 12/2011/QĐ-TTg promulgated by the Prime Minister: "The supporting industries are industries producing materials, spare parts, components, accessories or semi-finished products as the means of the production of final products in production and assembly industries or of consumer products" [21]. Accordingly, Decision No. 1483/QĐ-TTg promulgated by the Prime Minister, on August 26, 2011, stated: "On promulgating a list of supporting industry products that are given priority for development" [22], there are six industries which are identified, including textile-garments, leather shoes, electronic computing, manufacturing and assembly automobiles, mechanical engineering, and supporting industry products used for and by high-tech industries.

Supporting industries can play a role in promoting economic growth [7]. A country with competitive supporting industries will contribute to economic development and national welfare even in the long run [6]. It is expressed through the following means: First, the development of competitive supporting industries will cause the dynamic effect of promoting technological innovations and developing human resources, thereby improving national welfare [23]. Second, a country with competitive supporting industries can sustain FDI for final assembly processes relatively longer than a country without competitive supporting industries. And, finally, a country with competitive supporting industries can export manufactured inputs to countries where the final assembly processes are ultimately transferred. Moreover, it should be noted that national industries will benefit most when the domestic supporting industries are able to become globally competitive, although a nation does not need to be competitive in all supporting industries if it has specialization in certain given areas [24]. Therefore, developing countries may wish to establish competitive supporting industries for long-term economic growth.

As stated, Vietnam is a developing country, and the industrialization and modernization is still progressing [25–28]. Therefore, the Vietnamese government is concentrating on promoting supporting industries wherever possible. This promotion is exemplified by Vietnam's support of industry prospects currently under assessment by Japanese enterprises [18], coupled with various decisions and policies for developing supporting industries such as: Decision No. 34/2007/QD-BCN, promulgated on July 31, 2007, by the Minister of Industry and Trade, which states: "Approving the planning of industrial development supports up to 2010 and vision to 2020" [29]; Decision No. 12/2011/QD-TTg, promulgated on February 24, 2011, by the Prime Minister, which states: "On development policies of some supporting industries" [21]; Decision No. 1843//QD-TTg, promulgated on August 26, 2011, by the Prime Minister, which states: "On promulgating a list of supporting industry products that are given priority for development" [22]; Decision No. 1556/QD-TTg, promulgated on October 17, 2012, by the Prime Minister, which states: "Development of an approval scheme, to help developing small and medium enterprises in supporting industries field" [19]; Decision No. 9028/QD-BCT, promulgated on October 10, 2014, by the Minister of Industry and Trade, which states: "Approval of a master plan for developing supporting industries up to 2020, vision to 2030" [30]; Decree No. 1111/2015/ND-CP, promulgated on November 3, 2015, by the Prime Minister, which states: "On the development of supporting industries" [31]; Decision No. 68/QD-TTg, promulgated on January 18, 2017, by the Prime Minister, which states: "On the approving of the program on development of supporting industries from 2016 to 2025" [32]; Decision No. 10/2017/QD-TTg, promulgated on April 3, 2017, by the Prime Minister, which states: "Promulgating the regulation on management and implementation of the program on development of supporting industries" [33]; and Decision No. 4572/QD-BCT, promulgated on November 7, 2014, by the Minister of Industry and Trade, which states: "Promulgating the regulation on formulation, receipt, appraisal, approval and implementation of schemes under the program on development of supporting industries" [34]. However, Vietnam's supporting industries are still in the very initial stages of development. The reality of supporting industries in Vietnam is that they are significantly lower in developmental status and weak in competitiveness [35]. This is evidenced by the lower proportion of locally finished goods. One recent Vietnamese governmental report [36] and a notice from the General Statistics Office of Vietnam [8] indicate that the proportion of localization in finished products in some supporting industries is 10.5% in manufacturing and assembly of automobiles, 17.2% in electronics, 12.5% in mechanical engineering, 9.5% in textile-garments, and 13.1% in leather shoes. This obviously underdeveloped state of the local supporting industry has negatively resulted in increased production costs, the risk of bigger trade deficits with foreign partners, and a lowered competitiveness of Vietnamese products than regional peers. This is due in large part to the importation of components and spare parts, which continues to be one of the primary factors preventing industrial development and economic growth, leading to increased national welfare. Some of the major factors which have led to overall weakness in Vietnam's supporting industries are a lack of capital expenditure, reduced technological innovation, and paucity of management skills for development [2].

2.2 Strategy for attracting FDI for developing supporting industries

Developing countries may improve national welfare by attracting FDI [37]. It is understood that FDI supports economic growth, increased personal incomes, and leads to a greater rate of employment and technological transfer on a national basis [37]. Moreover, there are five main channels of technological diffusion which are linked to FDI flows: demonstration or imitation; labor mobility; exportation; competition; and backward and forward linkages with domestic firms [38]. These five channels, respectively, match the following situations: (i) the efforts of domestic firms to adopt successful technology used by multinational corporations (MNCs); (ii) the recruitment by domestic firms of workers with MNC experience who are able to use different technologies; (iii) access to large distribution networks and the related gain due to a better knowledge of consumer tastes in foreign markets; (iv) a more efficient usage of existing resources and technology or the incorporation by domestic firms of new technologies in the production process to compete with MNCs; and (v) the relationship between MNCs and domestic firms, where the latter can become suppliers of MNCs (backward linkages) or customers of intermediate outputs of MNCs (forward linkages) [37].

In addition, the research results produced by international case studies, in terms of the positive impact FDI flows have on the invested country, are related as follows: (i) managing the status of lack of funds and thereby increasing labor productivity, employment, and other production factors; (ii) promoting the growth by increasing total social investment; (iii) keeping the balance of payments; (iv) contributing to diversification of the production structure; (v) employment effects; and (vi) a transfer of technology [2]. The infusion of FDI creates the effect of future production and further investment both before and after subsequent production stages have been initiated. The general situation in many countries, Vietnam included, is that FDI significantly contributes to export growth and job creation, but it does not help to increase the level of national prosperity despite job creation, albeit at minimum wage, in the manufacturing sector. However, FDI flows may have the potential of causing major instability to a given marketplace environment, as follows: pinching domestic manufacturers instead of network cooperation and weakening the overall sense of prosperity through the outward transfer of profits and income to foreign countries. This situation would decidedly be in favor of the investors who make investments through massive incentive programs presented by host countries [17].

Many empirical studies support the theory that MNCs and MNEs tend to have higher productivity than domestic firms located in the same sector, thereby contributing to considerable GDP growth in developing markets. While customers of supporting industries are typically domestic assemblers, it is possible for foreign assemblers to become located in the domestic market and for foreign assemblers to also be located in adjacent foreign countries in the region [37]. It should be noted that foreign assemblers are frequently MNCs and MNEs. More importantly, it seems that developing countries expect that MNCs will have a supposed positive impact on the productivity levels of domestic firms by the potential generation of positive externalities. FDI may generate positive externalities worthy of the productivity growth of domestic suppliers through business relationships with MNCs (known as "backward linkages" afterward) and to increased output and productivity of domestic supporting industries, due to the additional demand and technological transfer caused by MNCs. Moreover, if increasing FDI causes positive externalities for domestic suppliers and concomitantly improves their productivity through backward linkages, national welfare in FDI host countries will also undoubtedly improve. Finally, developing countries may improve their national welfare through the attraction of FDI, if their supporting industries can obtain positive externalities that far exceed the negative externalities some domestic assemblers may yet encounter [2].

The role of FDI in the development of supporting industries is seen as follows: (i) to develop the infrastructure of the industry, paving the way for the development supporting industries; (ii) to expand the market scale; (iii) to create conditions for the host country to participate in global production networks, pushing them up to higher-value stage in the value chain; (iv) to implement the international division of labor and human resource development; and (v) to develop and transfer technology to the host country. Aside from the positive impacts, FDI may also negatively impact industry in invested countries, such as (1) pinching domestic manufacturers instead of meeting network needs, as in the case of foreign manufacturers who choose to produce supporting industry products as domestic enterprises, and (2) causing environmental pollution and depleting host country resources due to involvement with supporting industry small- and medium-sized enterprises using outdated technology or with TNCs' strategies which invest overseas solely for purposes of natural resource exploitation.

Accordingly, the importance of competitive supporting industries as partners in MNCs' dynamic technology innovation and their positive roles as the recipients of technology transfer from MNCs has been stressed [24]. Additionally, domestic supporting industries may wish to take advantage of their relative geographical proximity to MNCs for purposes of rapid information flow and technical interchange. Therefore, it is important to note that for developing countries to establish competitive supporting industries, FDI-driven economic growth must occur as a prerequisite. Furthermore, domestic supporting industries are of increasing importance because they may act as a significant factor to attract FDI as well [2]. In a reverse sense, FDI will promote the development of supporting industries. Thus, attracting FDI for the development of supporting industries motivates an economy's sustainable level of growth, thus stimulating the national technological development and increasing national competitiveness on a global scale.

Evaluation criteria useful for analyzing the attraction of FDI for the development of supporting industries may be considered, as follows:

First, FDI inflows on supporting industry: The increase or decrease in FDI flow into supporting industries reflects the attractiveness of supporting industries for FDI enterprises as well as for those countries that receive the FDI. So, the FDI inflows to supporting industries are considered to be part of the capital flow on implementation, the number of projects in each industry, and the scale of FDI enterprises in those supporting industries.

Secondly, technological transfer from FDI enterprises to supporting industry enterprises: It reflects the quality of supporting industries products as well as the ability to receive technological transfer from TNCs, MNCs, and MNEs of domestic enterprises.

Thirdly, the association level between FDI enterprises and domestic enterprises: It expresses a connection between both domestic and FDI enterprises. It should be considered from two aspects: (i) the relationship between supporting industries enterprises with customers and suppliers and (ii) the correlation between supplying resources of internal businesses, importing, and domestic supplying resources.

Fourthly, development of human resources and management skills: It is wholly transferrable through FDI exchange to the host country.

Finally, environmental problems: Strict environmental regulations will nurture technological development and facilitate the creation of a "green" technology market [39].

There are two trends which are known to attract FDI for the development of industry in developing countries. These trends include, but are not limited to, (1) attracting FDI in assembly-related industries before investment in component manufacturing industries since the development of an assembly industry will promote the development of a component manufacturing industry and other supporting industries (This is called a "linking effect" toward the inputs that will have an impact leading to the development of one industry with supporting industries in manufacturing intermediate inputs) and (2) attracting FDI in manufacturing industries before entering the component-assembling industry, so that the component manufacturing industry will develop before the assembly sector concerns; or, in other words, the development of a component industry will lead to the development of related assembly industries. As more and more facilities appear in an effort to supply intermediate equipment and materials, goods manufacturers and enterprises will soon have an even greater ability to access raw materials and component sources. Therefore, the average cost for manufacturing and assembling will decrease, and these countries shall continuously attract more multinational companies to set up new assembly plants at those relative locations [2].

Because of its status as a developing country, Vietnam has concentrated on attracting FDI to develop supporting industries. However, the attraction of FDI to develop supporting industries in Vietnam is still a weakness due to a deficient quantity of total governmental capital expenditure and qualitative infrastructure projects. The General Statistics Office of Vietnam [9] states that the total cumulative FDI for developing supporting industries is approximately US $29.7 billion, accounting for 16.8% quantity of FDI projects and 18.3% of the total FDI value in all supporting industries and main industries. This study examines the reality of developing supporting industries and attracting FDI for the development of supporting industries in Vietnam. The results indicate that there are eight important factors for making investment decisions by foreign investors whenever deciding to invest in Vietnam's supporting industries [6], including:

1. *Institutions and state policies*: This all-important factor creates just the right conditions for the development of supporting industries. The factorial impact may be expressed in two possible ways: First, it is the view of the state regarding the development of supporting industries to orient the national industrial development strategy to be consistent with the trend of globalization and international economic integration. The relationships needed to associate with the international economy must be expanded upon. It must be understood that the mutual assurance of relationships between supporting areas and industrial manufacturing sectors is not to be confined within a single country but within a regional or a global scale. Therefore, a unified view of any development regarding supporting industries is particularly important for national and industrial development of supporting industries to occur. Second, the policy on the development of industry and supporting industries in a country, which may or may not be developed, is largely dependent on the development strategies and policies decided by the state. Therefore, those policies related to promoting supporting industries, such as support for information technology, capital, provisions of association in business, etc., will greatly contribute to the promotional development of supporting industry. On the other hand, the localization policy; tax policy on importing and manufacturing semifinished products, both parts and components; the level of state-sponsored investment in scientific research and technology in supporting industry areas; the laws, standards, and technical regulations promulgated on behalf of industries; and diversification of products within the supporting industry networks can be seen to either facilitate or hinder the continued development of supporting industries. This is due in most part to the presence or the lack of a development-oriented perspective of the state as it is related to this issue [40, 41].

2. *Human resources:* Due to the manpower requirements of supporting industries, human resources are a principal factor maintaining a strong impact on future levels of industrial development and national supporting industries. The criteria of interest for determining human resources include the number, educational background, personal qualifications, absorptive capacity, self-discipline, communication skills (including language competency), drive for innovation, and professionalism of the human resources managers who are involved [2, 39, 42].

3. *Infrastructure facilities:* This remains an important influence needed to attract FDI for the development of strategic investment (SI). Any nation possessing appropriate infrastructure (i.e., transportation, power, information, and communication) conditions has an advantage in attracting FDI to develop supportive industries, while a lack of infrastructure means the opposite is inevitable [41].

4. *Domestic supply capability:* In order to ensure the domestic supply of materials, parts, and accessories for production-stage products derived from MNEs, the domestic supply chain (i.e., total value and partition of the domestic supply and the quantity and size of supporting industry firms) must have a huge number of offerings at its disposal, good quality, and cheap prices. It will greatly help MNEs to minimize the costs incurred for transportation and storage while guaranteeing the timely delivery through accurate production planning and the timely assembly of MNEs [43].

5. *Market size of supporting industries:* Market size (i.e., total consumption of supporting industries products) and outsourced procurement both play a central role in the development of SI. If a market is large enough to attract business participation in the supply of products and services, it will enable MNEs to easily facilitate partnership, make technology transfers possible, and establish business linkages [43].

6. *Technological development and innovation:* As a solid foundation for the development of principal industry, supporting industries require considerable regular investment in terms of modern machinery, capital equipment, and innovative technology. Assemblage enterprises consistently set out many stringent requirements for the technical standards involved in the production of component types and spare parts. Therefore, if the supporting enterprises do not apply modern technology and improved techniques in their manufacturing efforts, they will not be able to create products which match assemblers' exacting standards. At such a time, the assemblers will have to invest in the manufacturing of, or importation of, overseas components and parts by themselves to meet client needs [2, 18].

7. *International cooperation and competition:* The liberalization of trade and investment, through international forums and region, significantly reduces transaction costs, increases trade, and strengthens national competitiveness and international engagement. Moreover, the level of competition in attracting investment capital between countries is becoming ever more acute as global revenue pools shrink. To enhance competitiveness in attracting FDI, a growing number of countries have tried to adjust their national policies and to improve the local investment climate to become more attractive for foreign investment to occur [6].

8. *Other criteria*: The influence of attracting FDI toward the overall development of supporting industries is important. This factor (i.e., environment policy, culture, tax policy, land supporting, corruption, inclusion of MNEs) will lead to a positive ripple effect in the national economy, which, in turn, will lead to further employment opportunities, greater tax digest, and sustainable growth for the host nation [6].

When taken together, there are various alternative strategy policies possible for attracting FDI to develop supporting industries, namely: (1) attracting FDI for developing supporting industries, which motivates the economy's sustainable growth; (2) attracting FDI for developing supporting industries, which increases national competitiveness; and (3) attracting FDI for developing supporting industries, which stimulates the nation's technological development, leading to significant benefits overall.

3. Research methodology

Respective of this study, the proposed procedure utilizes the consistent fuzzy preference relations (CFPR) process to select a beneficial strategy for attracting foreign direct investment (FDI). The following section will give a brief description of the suggested CFPR method.

Herrera-Viedma et al. [9] proposed the consistent fuzzy preference relations methodology in accordance with two preference relations, namely, the multiplicative preference relation and fuzzy preference relation (10)–(16).

3.1 Multiplicative preference relations

A multiplicative preference relations A on a set of alternatives X is represented by a preference relations matrix $A \subset \mathrm{X} \times \mathrm{X}$, $A = (a_{ij})$, $a_{ij} \in \left[\frac{1}{9}, 9\right]$, where a_{ij} denotes the ratio of the preference degree of alternative x_i over x_j [44, 45]. As $a_{ij} = 1$ indicates no difference between x_i and x_j, $a_{ij} = 9$ indicates that x_i is strongly preferable to x_j. A is assumed to be a multiplicative reciprocal, that is,

$$a_{ij} \cdot a_{ji} = 1 \forall i, j \in \{1, \ldots, n\} \tag{1}$$

Definition 3.1. A reciprocal multiplicative preference relation $A = (a_{ij})$ is consistent if.

$$a_{ij} \cdot a_{jk} = \mathrm{a}_{ik} \forall i, j, k = 1, \ldots, n \tag{2}$$

3.2 Fuzzy preference relation

Expert preferences over a set of alternatives where X is denoted by a positive preference relation matrix $P \subset X \times X$ with membership function $\beta_p : X \times X \rightarrow [0, 1]$, where $p_{ij} = \beta_p(x_i, x_j)$ indicates the ratio of the preference intensity of alternative x_i to that of x_j. Moreover, if $p_{ij} = \sum_{i=1}^{n} p_{ij}$ implies indifference between x_i and x_j ($x_i \sim x_j$), $p_{ij} = 1$ indicates that x_i is absolutely preferred to x_j, $p_{ij} = 0$ indicates x_j is absolutely preferred to x_i, and $p_{ij} > \frac{1}{2}$ indicates that x_i is preferred to x_i, $x_i > x_j$. Meanwhile, P is assumed to be an additive reciprocal, that is,

$$p_{ij} + p_{ji} = 1 \forall i, j \in \{1, \ldots, n\} \tag{3}$$

Proposition 3.1. Suppose that this paper has a set of alternatives, $X = \{x_1, \dots, x_n\}$, and associated with it is a reciprocal multiplicative preference relation $A = (a_{ij})$ with $a_{ij} \in \left[\frac{1}{9}, 9\right]$. Then, the corresponding reciprocal fuzzy preference relation, $P = \left(p_{ij}\right)$, with $p_{ij} \in [0, 1]$ associated with A is given as follows:

$$p_{ij} = g(a_{ij}) = \frac{1}{2} \cdot (1 + \log_9 a_{ij}) \tag{4}$$

With such a transformation function g, this paper can relate the research issues obtained for both kinds of preference relations.

3.3 On consistency of the fuzzy preference relations

Proposition 3.2. Let $A = (a_{ij})$ be a consistent multiplicative preference relation; then the corresponding reciprocal fuzzy preference relations $P = g(A)$ verify additive transitivity property.

Proof. For $A = (a_{ij})$ being consistent, this paper has that $a_{ij} \cdot a_{jk} = a_{ik} \forall i, j, k$ or equivalently $a_{ij} \cdot a_{jk} \cdot a_{ki} = 1 \, \forall i, j, k$. Taking logarithms on both sides, it has.

$$\log_9 a_{ij} + \log_9 a_{jk} + \log_9 a_{ki} = 0 \forall i, j, k \tag{5}$$

Adding 3 to both sides and dividing by 2 yields.

$$\frac{1}{2} \cdot (1 + \log_9 a_{ij}) + \frac{1}{2} \cdot (1 + \log_9 a_{jk}) + \frac{1}{2} \cdot (1 + \log_9 a_{ki}) = \frac{3}{2} \forall i, j, k \tag{6}$$

The fuzzy preference relations $P = g(A)$, being $p_{ij} = \frac{1}{2} \cdot (1 + \log_9 a_{ij})$, verifies.

$$p_{ij} + p_{jk} + p_{ik} = \frac{3}{2} \forall i, j, k \tag{7}$$

We conclude that $P = g(A)$ verifies additive transitivity property.

In such a way, this paper considers the following definition of the consistent fuzzy preference relation:

Definition 3.3. A reciprocal fuzzy preference relation $P = (p_{ij})$ is consistent if.

$$p_{ij} + p_{jk} + p_{ki} = \frac{3}{2} \forall i, j, k = 1, \dots n \tag{8}$$

In what follows, this paper will use the term additive consistency to refer to consistency for fuzzy preference relations based on the additive transitivity property.

3.4 Additive transitivity consistency of the fuzzy preference relations

Proposition 3.4-1. For a reciprocal fuzzy preference relation $P = (p_{ij})$, the following statements are equivalent:

$$\text{i. } p_{ij} + p_{jk} + p_{ki} = \frac{3}{2} \forall i, j, k \tag{9}$$

$$\text{ii. } p_{ij} + p_{jk} + p_{ki} = \frac{3}{2} \forall i < j < k \tag{10}$$

Proposition 3.4-2. A fuzzy preference relation $P = (p_{ij})$ is consistent if and only if.

$$p_{ij} + p_{jk} + p_{ki} = \frac{3}{2} \forall i \leq j \leq k \tag{11}$$

Proposition 3.4-3. For a reciprocal additive fuzzy preference relation $P = (p_{ij})$, the following statements are equivalent:

$$\text{i. } p_{ij} + p_{jk} + p_{ki} = \frac{3}{2} \forall i < j < k \tag{12}$$

$$\text{ii. } p_{i(i+1)} + p_{(i+1)(i+2)} + \dots p_{(j-1)j} + p_{ji} = \frac{j-i+1}{2} \forall i < j \tag{13}$$

3.5 Construct a consistency of the fuzzy preference relations

If the preference matrix contains any values that are not in the interval $[0, 1]$, but in an interval $[-a, 1+a]$, being $a > 0$, a linear solution is required to preserve the reciprocity and additive transitivity, that is, $F : [-a, 1+a] \to [0, 1]$. Therefore, by Proposition 3.4, it can construct a consistent fuzzy preference relation P' on $X = \{x_1, x_2, \dots, x_n; n \geq 2\}$ from $n - 1$ preference values $\{p_{12}, p_{23}, \dots, p_{n-1n}\}$; the steps are described in the following:

1. Compute the set of preference values B as

$$B = \left\{p_{ij}, i < j \wedge p_{ij} \notin \{p_{12}, p_{23}, \dots, p_{n-1n}\}\right\}; p_{ij} = \frac{j-i+1}{2} - p_{ii+1} - p_{i+1i+2} - p_{j-1j} \tag{14}$$

$$a = \left| \min\left\{B \cup \{p_{12}, p_{23}, \dots, p_{n-1n}\}\right\}\right| \tag{15}$$

$$P = \{p_{12}, p_{23}, \dots, p_{n-1n}\} \cup B \cup \{1 - p_{12}, 1 - p_{23}, \dots, 1 - p_{n-1n}\} \cup \neg B \tag{16}$$

2. The consistent fuzzy preference relation P′ is obtained as $P' = f(P)$ such that

$$f : [-a, 1+a] \to [0, 1] \tag{17}$$

$$f(x) = \frac{x+a}{1+2a} \tag{18}$$

4. Framework for selecting a strategy for attracting FDI under multi-criteria decision-making

4.1 Evaluated criteria and framework of the evaluation model

As part of this study, 22 government staff members and policy-makers, foreign investors, managers of 6 supporting industries, and economists were interviewed in order to examine the current status of developing supporting industries and attracting FDI for developing supporting industries in Vietnam.

Their identifications and their attributes are summarized as follows: C_1, institutions and policies; C_2, human resources; C_3, infrastructure facilities; C_4, domestic supply capability; C_5, market size of supporting industries (total consumption of supporting industries' products); C_6, technological development and innovation; C_7, international cooperation and competition; and C_8, other criteria.

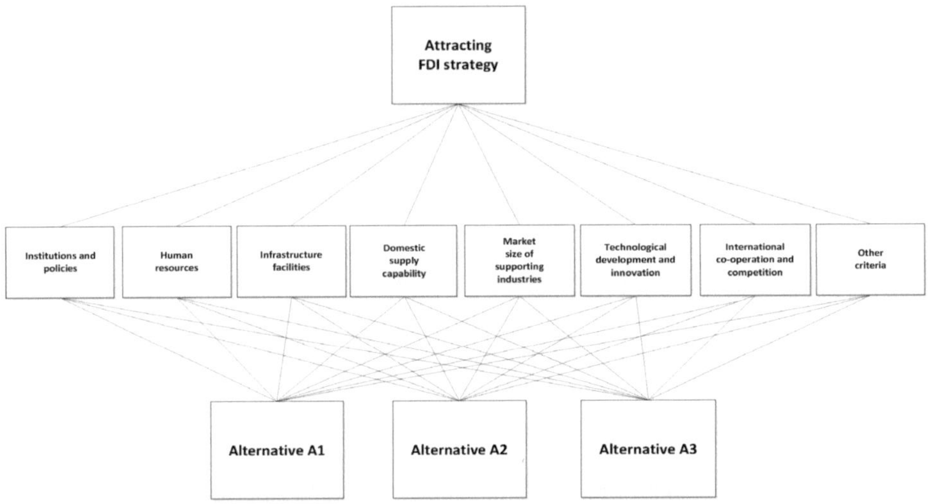

Figure 1.
Analytical framework to select a strategy for attracting FDI for Vietnam's supporting industries.

Following the analytical framework, there are candidate solutions for identifying the strategy useful toward attracting FDI and that will eventually develop supporting industries. These include attracting FDI for developing supporting industries, which motivates the economy's sustainable growth (A_1); attracting FDI for developing supporting industries, which increases national competitiveness (A_2); and attracting FDI for developing supporting industries, which stimulates the national technological development (A_3), respectively. An analytical hierarchy framework based on eight main criteria and three alternatives is established in **Figure 1**.

4.2 Hierarchical analytical process for selection of a strategy attracting FDI

4.2.1 Linguistic variables

This study compares certain pairs of criteria using expressions such as "equally important (EQ)," "moderately important (MO)," "strongly important (ST)," "very strongly important (VS)," and "absolutely important (AB)," using a 5-point Likert-type scale possessing values indicated by actual numbers (see **Table 1**).

Additionally, three linguistic variables, namely, "very high (VH)," "high (H)," and "fair (F)," are used to measure the strategy for attracting FDI to develop supporting industries in Vietnam (see **Table 2**).

Definition	Intensity of importance
Equally important (EQ)	1
Moderate important (MO)	3
Strongly important (ST)	5
Very strongly important (VS)	7
Absolutely important (AB)	9
Intermediate values between two adjacent judgments	2, 4, 6, 8

Table 1.
Linguistic terms for priority weights of influential factors to attract FDI.

Definition	Intensity of importance
Fair (F)	1
High (H)	3
Very high (VH)	5
Intermediate values use to present compromise	2, 4

Table 2.
Linguistic variables for the priority rating of attracting FDI strategy.

4.2.2 Reciprocal additive consistent fuzzy preference relations for prioritizing the evaluation criteria

AHP separates a complex decision issue into elemental problems to produce a hierarchical model. Each of these preference relations necessitates the completion of all $\frac{n\cdot(n+1)}{2}$ judgments for a preference matrix containing n elements. To reduce the judgment times, this study employs the reciprocal additive consistent fuzzy preference relation designed by Herrera-Viedma et al. [9] because it requires only $n-1$ judgments from a set of n elements.

The procedures of the reciprocal additive consistent fuzzy preference relations for prioritizing the assessment criteria are given below:

1. Establish pairwise comparison matrices among all of the criteria $(C_i, i = 1, 2, \dots, n)$ in the dimensions of the hierarchy system. The evaluators $(E_k, k = 1, 2, \dots, m)$ provide the more important of each of the pairs of considered criteria for a set of n-1 preference values $\left(a_{12}, a_{23}, \dots, a_{(n-1)n}\right)$, for

$$A^k = \begin{matrix} & \begin{matrix} C_1 & C_2 & \cdots & C_{n-1} & C_n \end{matrix} \\ \begin{matrix} C_1 \\ C_2 \\ \vdots \\ C_{n-1} \\ C_n \end{matrix} & \begin{bmatrix} 1 & a_{12}^k & \cdots & x & x \\ x & 1 & a_{23}^k & x & x \\ \vdots & \vdots & \ddots & \ddots & \vdots \\ x & x & \cdots & 1 & a_{n-1n}^k \\ x & x & \cdots & x & 1 \end{bmatrix} \end{matrix} \quad (19)$$

where a_{ij}^k denotes the preference intensity toward considered criteria i and j, which are assessed by evaluator k; $a_{ij} = 1$ indicates no difference between considered criteria i and j; $a_{ij} = 3, 5, 7, 9$ reveals that criterion i is relatively important to criterion j; and $a_{ij} = \frac{1}{3}, \frac{1}{5}, \frac{1}{7}, \frac{1}{9}$ indicates that considered criterion i is less important than criterion j. The sign "x" indicates the remaining a_{ij}^k, which can be done via inverse comparison.

2. Transform the preference value a_{ij}^k into p_{ij}^k using an interval scale $[0, 1]$, and then derive the remaining p_{ij}^k based on the reciprocal transitivity property, as follows:

$$P^k = \frac{1}{2}(1+\log_9 A^k) = \begin{array}{c} \\ C_1 \\ C_2 \\ \vdots \\ C_n \end{array} \begin{array}{c} \begin{array}{cccc} C_1 & C_2 & \dots & C_n \end{array} \\ \begin{bmatrix} 0.5 & p_{12}^k & x & x \\ x & 0.5 & p_{23}^k & x \\ \vdots & \vdots & \vdots & \vdots \\ x & x & \dots & 0.5 \end{bmatrix} \end{array} \tag{20}$$

where $p_{ij} = 0.5$ indicates no difference between criteria i and j, $p_{ij} = 1$ demonstrates that criterion i is absolutely important to criterion j, and $p_{ij} = 0$ illustrates that criterion i is absolutely less important to criterion j. The remaining p_{ij}^k can be calculated using Eqs. (3) and (13), but in an interval $[-a, 1+a]$, and a transformation function is required to preserve the reciprocity and additive transitivity. The transformation function is

$$f\left(p_{ij}^k\right) = \frac{p_{ij}^k + a}{1 + 2 \cdot a} \tag{21}$$

where a denotes the absolute value of the minimum negative value or maximum positive value minus one in this preference matrix.

3. The study pulled the opinions of evaluators to obtain the aggregated weights of the criteria. Moreover, let p_{ij}^k denote the transformed fuzzy preference value of evaluator k for assessing the criteria i and j. This study uses the notation of the average value to integrate the judgment values of m evaluators, namely,

$$p_{ij} = \left(p_{ij}^1 + p_{ij}^2 + \dots + p_{ij}^m\right)/m \tag{22}$$

4. Normalizing the aggregated fuzzy preference relation matrices q_{ij} is used to indicate the normalized fuzzy preference values of each considered criteria, such as

$$q_{ij} = p_{ij} / \sum_{i=1}^{n} p_{ij} \tag{23}$$

5. Using the ϖ_i denoting the average priority weight of considered criterion i, the priority of each criterion can be obtained, that is,

$$\varpi_i = \frac{1}{n} \cdot \sum_{i=1}^{n} q_{ij} \tag{24}$$

where n denotes the number of criteria considered.

4.2.3 Obtaining the synthetic utility value for a strategy attracting FDI with respect to each criterion

The evaluators were asked to express their subjective judgments regarding the preference ratings of a strategy for attracting FDI $(A_r, r = 1, 2, \dots, s)$ with respect to each considered criteria in linguistic terms.

1. For each considered criteria, the evaluators were asked to choose the best among three attracting FDI strategies for a set of $s-1$ preference data $(o_{12}, o_{23}, \dots, o_{(s-1)s})$, for example,

$$
{}_iG = \begin{array}{c} \\ A_1 \\ A_2 \\ \vdots \\ A_s \end{array}
\begin{array}{c} \begin{array}{cccc} A_1 & A_2 & \cdots & A_s \end{array} \\
\begin{bmatrix} 1 & {}_ig_{12}^k & x & x \\ x & 1 & {}_ig_{23}^k & x \\ \vdots & \vdots & \vdots & {}_ig_{(s-1)s}^k \\ x & x & \cdots & 1 \end{bmatrix} \end{array} \tag{25}
$$

where ${}_io_{rt}^k$ represents the performance value assigned by evaluator k to attract FDI strategy r and t based on considered criterion i.

2. Next, the preference value ${}_io_{rt}^k$ is transformed within the range $\left[\frac{1}{5}, 5\right]$ into ${}_iu_{rt}^k$ in an interval scale $[0, 1]$, and the remaining ${}_iu_{rt}^k$ are obtained via the reciprocal transitivity property as follows:

$$
{}_iQ = \frac{1}{2}(1+\log_5 {}_iG) = \begin{array}{c} \\ A_1 \\ A_2 \\ \vdots \\ A_s \end{array}
\begin{array}{c} \begin{array}{cccc} A_1 & A_2 & \cdots & A_s \end{array} \\
\begin{bmatrix} 0.5 & {}_iq_{12}^k & x & x \\ x & 0.5 & {}_iq_{23}^k & x \\ \vdots & \vdots & \vdots & {}_iq_{(s-1)s}^k \\ x & x & \cdots & 0.5 \end{bmatrix} \end{array} \tag{26}
$$

3. The opinions of evaluators are then taken to obtain the transformed synthetic rating of the strategy for attracting FDI for each considered criteria ${}_iu_{rt}^k$ which denotes the transformed fuzzy preference value of evaluator k for assessing strategies for attracting FDI r and t in terms of considered criterion i. This study uses the notation of average value to integrate the judgment values of m evaluators, that is,

$$
{}_iu_{rt} = \frac{1}{m} \cdot \sum_{j=1}^{m} {}_iu_{rt}^k \tag{27}
$$

4. Following the normalization of the synthetic fuzzy preference rating of the strategy for attracting FDI for each considered criteria, ${}_i\alpha_{rt}$ is adopted to indicate the normalized rating of the strategies for attracting FDI u and v with respect to considered criterion i, for example,

$$
{}_i\alpha_{rt} = {}_iu_{rt} / \sum_{r=1}^{s} {}_iu_{rt} \tag{28}
$$

5. Consequently, ${}_i\overline{\beta}_r$ denotes the average rating of the strategy for attracting FDI r with respect to considered criterion i. The desired rating of each strategy for attracting FDI can be derived for each considered criterion, that is,

$$
{}_i\overline{\beta}_r = \frac{1}{s} \cdot \sum_{t=1}^{s} \alpha_{rt} \tag{29}
$$

where s represents the number of the strategy for attracting FDI.

4.2.4 Obtaining the priority weight for selection

A preferred value U_r for developing supporting industries in Vietnam is obtained by multiplying the priority weights of considered criteria by the ratings of the strategy for attracting FDI. That is,

$$U_r = \sum_{i=1}^{n} {}_i\overline{\beta}_r \cdot \varpi_i \mathrm{R_u} = \sum\nolimits_i \bar{\mathrm{l}}_{\mathrm{u}} * \varpi_{\mathrm{i}} \tag{30}$$

where ϖ_i denotes the aggregated weight of considered criterion i.

5. Results

This study used six supporting industries in Vietnam to serve as examples to demonstrate the efficacy of the theoretical framework proposed in this study. A total of 22 questionnaires were dispatched and effectively returned, with survey candidates including managers from the Vietnamese Local Industry Department and the Vietnamese Foreign Investment Agency, policy-makers, economists, foreign investors, and managers from representatives of the six supporting industries located in Vietnam.

5.1 Weighting calculation of the evaluating criteria

Eight major evaluation criteria are considered as part of the problem of selecting a strategy for attracting FDI considered herein. The pairwise comparisons for these eight criteria are obtained by means of interviews with the assessment representatives involved in this study.

The following examples clarify the computational process used to derive the priority weights using the reciprocal additive consistent fuzzy preference relation approach:

1. Based on the interviews taken with the 22 representatives regarding the relative importance of eight aforementioned evaluation criteria, **Table 3** lists the pairwise comparison matrices for a set of $n-1$ neighboring criteria $\{a_{12}, a_{23}, \ldots, a_{78}\}$ with their corresponding numbers.

2. The assessment of evaluator 1 (E_1) may serve as an example, and it is listed in **Table 4**. Also listed are the linguistic terms, which are transferrable into corresponding numbers.

3. Eq. (4) was used to transform the elements (listed in **Table 4**) into an interval $[0, 1]$, yielding the following values:

$$p_{12} = (1+\log_9 9.0000)/2 = 1.0000;\ p_{23} = (1+\log_9 5.0000)/2 = 0.8662;$$
$$p_{34} = (1+\log_9 0.2500)/2 = 0.1845;\ p_{45} = (1+\log_9 7.0000)/2 = 0.8662;$$
$$p_{56} = (1+\log_9 0.3333)/2 = 0.2500;\ p_{67} = (1+\log_9 7.0000)/2 = 0.9428;$$
$$p_{78} = (1+\log_9 3.0000)/2 = 0.7500.$$

The remaining value then can be calculated using Eqs. (3) and (13) with $p_{21}, p_{31}, p_{81}, p_{82}, p_{28}$, etc., being used as examples:

DOI: http://dx.doi.org/10.5772/intechopen.90125

	E_1	E_2	E_3	E_4	E_5	E_6	E_7	E_8	E_9	E_{10}	E_{11}	E_{12}	E_{13}	E_{14}	E_{15}	E_{16}	E_{17}	E_{18}	E_{19}	E_{20}	E_{21}	E_{22}	
C_1	9	9	7	8	3	9	6	4	9	8	5	7	9	7	5	9	7	8	6	9	5	8	C_2
C_2	5	6	5	6	2	5	4	3	6	5	4	5	7	4	3	7	6	5	4	5	4	5	C_3
C_3	1/4	1/7	1/4	1/6	1/4	1/7	1/1	1/5	1/4	1/6	¼	1/5	1/7	1/5	1/4	1/6	1/5	1/5	1/4	1/6	1/5	1/3	C_4
C_4	5	8	6	7	4	8	5	4	8	7	5	7	8	6	5	7	8	7	5	8	5	6	C_5
C_5	1/3	1/2	1/4	1/3	2	1/3	1	1/2	1	1/2	1	1/3	12	1/2	1/3	1	1/2	2	1/3	1	1/3	½	C_6
C_6	7	8	7	8	5	7	5	6	8	7	6	7	8	6	5	8	8	7	6	7	6	5	C_7
C_7	3	3	1/2	2	1	1/2	1	2	2	1	½	3	2	2	1	1/3	3	1	1/2	2	2	1	C_8

Table 3.
The linguistic terms into corresponding numbers toward eight factors assessed by evaluators.

E_1	C_1	C_2	C_3	C_4	C_5	C_6	C_7	C_8
C_1	1.0000	9.0000	x	x	x	x	x	x
C_2	x	1.0000	5.0000	x	x	x	x	x
C_3	x	x	1.0000	0.2500	x	x	x	x
C_4	x	x	x	1.0000	5.0000	x	x	x
C_5	x	x	x	x	1.0000	0.3333	x	x
C_6	x	x	x	x	x	1.0000	7.0000	x
C_7	x	x	x	x	x	x	1.0000	3.0000
C_8	x	x	x	x	x	x	x	1.0000

Where x is a variable that can be calculated using Eqs. (3) and (13).

Table 4.
Interval pairwise comparisons of the criteria.

$$p_{21} = 1 - p_{12} = 1 - 1.0000 = 0.0000;$$

$$p_{31} = \frac{3-1+1}{2} - p_{12} - p_{23} = 1.5 - 1.0000 - 0.8662 = -0.3662;$$

$$\begin{aligned} p_{81} &= \frac{8-1+1}{2} - p_{12} - p_{23} - p_{34} - p_{45} - p_{56} - p_{67} - p_{78} \\ &= 4 - 1.0000 - 0.8662 - 0.1845 - 0.8662 - 0.2500 - 0.9428 - 0.7500 = -0.8598 \end{aligned};$$

$$\begin{aligned} p_{82} &= \frac{8-2+1}{2} - p_{23} - p_{34} - p_{45} - p_{56} - p_{67} - p_{78} \\ &= 3.5 - 0.8662 - 0.1845 - 0.8662 - 0.2500 - 0.9428 - 0.7500 = -0.3598 \end{aligned};$$

$$p_{28} = 1 - p_{82} = 1 - (-0.3598) = 1.3598;$$

The fuzzy preference relation matrix for the eight evaluation criteria assessed by evaluator 1 is established in **Table 5**.

Table 5 lists $p_{13}, p_{14}, p_{15}, p_{16}, p_{17}, p_{18}, p_{27}, p_{28}, p_{31}, p_{41}, p_{47}, p_{48}, p_{51}, p_{61}, p_{68}, p_{71}, p_{72}, p_{74}, p_{81}, p_{82}, p_{84}$, and p_{86} elements but not in the interval [0, 1]; and thus a linear transformation stated in Eq. (21) is employed to ensure the reciprocity and additive transitivity for the preference relation matrix. **Table 6** lists the transformation matrix.

4. Likewise, the above computational procedures can calculate the fuzzy preference relation matrices of the other 21 evaluators; therefore, using Eq. (22), the aggregated pairwise comparison matrix of 22 evaluators can be derived, as listed in **Table 7**.

5. Eq. (23) is applied to normalize the aggregated pairwise comparison matrix. Taking q_{11} as an example:

q_{11} = 0.5000/(0.5000 + 0.3245 + 0.1859 + 0.3324 + 0.1659 + 0.2172 + 0.0434 + 0.0333) = 0.2774.

The priority weight of each evaluation criterion can then be obtained by Eq. (24). The priority weight and rank of each influence is assessed by 22 evaluators as listed in **Table 8**.

The ranks of the evaluation criteria weights thus are substituted as:

$C_1(0.2022) > C_4(0.1551) > C_2(0.1529) > C_6(0.1227) > C_3(0.1139) > C_5(0.1083) > C_7(0.0738) > C_8(0.0710)$.

The results show that the six main assessment attributes are institutions and policies (0.2022), domestic supply capacity (0.1551), human resources (0.1529), technological development and innovation (0.1227), infrastructure facilities

E_1	C_1	C_2	C_3	C_4	C_5	C_6	C_7	C_8
C_1	0.5000	1.0000	1.3662	1.0508	1.4170	1.1670	1.6098	1.8598
C_2	0.0000	0.5000	0.8662	0.5508	0.9170	0.6670	1.1098	1.3598
C_3	−0.3662	0.1338	0.5000	0.1845	0.5508	0.3008	0.7436	0.9936
C_4	−0.0508	0.4492	0.8155	0.5000	0.8662	0.6162	1.0590	1.3090
C_5	−0.4170	0.0830	0.4492	0.1338	0.5000	0.2500	0.6928	0.9424
C_6	−0.1670	0.3330	0.6992	0.3838	0.7500	0.5000	0.9428	1.1928
C_7	−0.6098	−0.1098	0.2564	−0.0590	0.3072	0.0572	0.5000	0.7500
C_8	−0.8598	−0.3598	0.0064	−0.3090	0.0572	−0.1928	0.2500	0.5000

Table 5.
Consistent fuzzy preference relations matrix of criteria E_1.

E_1	C_1	C_2	C_3	C_4	C_5	C_6	C_7	C_8
C_1	0.5000	0.6834	0.8185	0.7025	0.8372	0.7453	0.9081	1.0000
C_2	0.3162	0.5000	0.6347	0.5187	0.6533	0.5614	0.7242	0.8162
C_3	0.1815	0.3653	0.5000	0.3840	0.5187	0.4267	0.5896	0.6815
C_4	0.2975	0.4813	0.6160	0.5000	0.6347	0.5427	0.7056	0.7975
C_5	0.1628	0.3467	0.4813	0.3653	0.5000	0.4081	0.5709	0.6628
C_6	0.2547	0.4386	0.5733	0.4573	0.5919	0.5000	0.6628	0.7547
C_7	0.0919	0.2758	0.4104	0.2944	0.4291	0.3372	0.5000	0.5919
C_8	0.0000	0.1838	0.3185	0.2025	0.3372	0.2453	0.4081	0.5000

Table 6.
The transformation matrix of criteria by linear solution.

E	C_1	C_2	C_3	C_4	C_5	C_6	C_7	C_8
C_1	0.5000	0.6755	0.8141	0.6676	0.8341	0.7828	0.9566	0.9667
C_2	0.3245	0.5000	0.6385	0.4921	0.6586	0.6073	0.7811	0.7911
C_3	0.1859	0.3615	0.5000	0.3536	0.5201	0.4687	0.6425	0.6526
C_4	0.3324	0.5079	0.6464	0.5000	0.6665	0.6151	0.7889	0.7990
C_5	0.1659	0.3414	0.4799	0.3335	0.5000	0.4487	0.6225	0.6326
C_6	0.2172	0.3927	0.5313	0.3849	0.5513	0.5000	0.6738	0.6839
C_7	0.0434	0.2189	0.3575	0.2111	0.3775	0.3262	0.5000	0.5101
C_8	0.0333	0.2089	0.3474	0.2010	0.3674	0.3161	0.4899	0.5000
Total	1.8026	3.2068	4.3151	3.1438	4.4756	4.0649	5.4553	5.5360

Table 7.
Aggregated pairwise comparison matrices of the 22 evaluators.

E	C_1	C_2	C_3	C_4	C_5	C_6	C_7	C_8	Total	Weight	Ranking
C_1	0.2774	0.2107	0.1887	0.2124	0.1864	0.1926	0.1754	0.1746	1.6180	0.2022	1
C_2	0.1800	0.1559	0.1480	0.1565	0.1472	0.1494	0.1432	0.1429	1.2231	0.1529	3
C_3	0.1032	0.1127	0.1159	0.1125	0.1162	0.1153	0.1178	0.1179	0.9114	0.1139	5
C_4	0.1844	0.1584	0.1498	0.1590	0.1489	0.1513	0.1446	0.1443	1.2408	0.1551	2
C_5	0.0920	0.1065	0.1112	0.1061	0.1117	0.1104	0.1141	0.1143	0.8663	0.1083	6
C_6	0.1205	0.1225	0.1231	0.1224	0.1232	0.1230	0.1235	0.1235	0.9818	0.1227	4
C_7	0.0241	0.0683	0.0828	0.0671	0.0844	0.0802	0.0917	0.0921	0.5907	0.0738	7
C_8	0.0185	0.0651	0.0805	0.0639	0.0821	0.0778	0.0898	0.0903	0.5680	0.0710	8
Total	1.0000	1.0000	1.0000	1.0000	1.0000	1.0000	1.0000	1.0000	8.0000	1.0000	

Table 8.
Normalized matrix of priority weight and rank of influential factors.

(0.1139), and market size of supporting industries (0.1083). Meanwhile, the two least important attributes are international cooperation and competition (0.0738) and other criteria (0.0710).

5.2 Calculation of the weights for a strategy attracting FDI with respect to evaluation criteria

To determine the priority weight matrix for a strategy to attract FDI with respect to each evaluation criterion, **Table 2** lists the linguistic variables for evaluators. The priority weights of the three attractive FDI strategies are calculated as follows:

1. This study examines the implementation of this strategy for attracting FDI for developing supporting industries; the 22 evaluators are interviewed to assess which path is more likely to occur according to each evaluation criteria. **Table 9** lists the opinions of these 22 evaluators regarding their preference intensities related to the strategy for attracting FDI with respect to each evaluation criterion, and the linguistic term is assigned into the corresponding numbers.

2. The study uses this function, $p_{ij} = \frac{1}{2}(1 + \log_5 a_{ij})$, to transform the values in the scale $\left[\frac{1}{5}, 5\right]$ into the interval [0, 1]. **Table 10** lists the transformed preference data.

3. Using Eq. (27), and taking ${}_1u_{rt}$ as an example, the synthetic rating of a strategy for attracting FDI can be obtained (as listed in **Table 11**), where ${}_1u_{rt}$ represented the transformed fuzzy preference value of 22 evaluators for assessing strategies for r and t for attracting FDI in terms of evaluating criteria 1. Eqs. (28) and (29) can then be employed to normalize and synthesize the fuzzy preference rating of 3 attracting FDI strategies based on eight evaluation criteria. **Table 12** lists the normalized values and priority weights, while **Table 13** lists the normalized values and priority weights of all of the criteria.

5.3 Weighting the selection priorities

Using Eq. (30), the priority weights of the eight evaluation criteria and the priority ratings of three strategies for attracting FDI are given, in addition to the preference weightings of the candidates. They are listed in **Table 13**. The preferred weights for the strategy for attracting FDI are calculated as follows:

$$\begin{aligned} A_1 &= 0.2022 * 0.4405 + 0.1529 * 0.4396 + 0.1139 * 0.4378 + 0.1551 * 0.4427 \\ &\quad + 0.1083 * 0.4290 + 0.1227 * 0.4318 + 0.0738 * 0.4366 + 0.0710 * 0.4354 \\ &= 0.4374 \end{aligned}$$

$$\begin{aligned} A_2 &= 0.2022 * 0.2441 + 0.1529 * 0.2333 + 0.1139 * 0.2292 + 0.1551 * 0.2238 \\ &\quad + 0.1083 * 0.2367 + 0.1227 * 0.2236 + 0.0738 * 0.2321 + 0.0710 * 0.2247 \\ &= 0.2320 \end{aligned}$$

$$\begin{aligned} A_3 &= 0.2022 * 0.3155 + 0.1529 * 0.3271 + 0.1139 * 0.3330 + 0.1551 * 0.3335 \\ &\quad + 0.1083 * 0.3343 + 0.1227 * 0.3446 + 0.0738 * 0.3312 + 0.0710 * 0.3399 \\ &= 0.3306 \end{aligned}$$

From **Table 13**, the ranking of alternative solutions is obtained as follows: Alternative A_1 (0.4374) > alternative A_3 (0.3306) > alternative A_2 (0.2320). Evaluators clearly believe that the best policy for creating and implementing a strategy to

		E_1	E_2	E_3	E_4	E_5	E_6	E_7	E_8	E_9	E_{10}	E_{11}	E_{12}	E_{13}	E_{14}	E_{15}	E_{16}	E_{17}	E_{18}	E_{19}	E_{20}	E_{21}	E_{22}	
C_1	A_1	2.0000	3.0000	2.0000	4.0000	2.0000	5.0000	3.0000	4.0000	3.0000	3.0000	4.0000	2.0000	4.0000	1.0000	2.0000	3.0000	3.0000	1.0000	3.0000	4.0000	0.5000	4.0000	A_2
	A_2	0.5000	1.0000	0.2500	2.0000	0.3333	0.5000	1.0000	2.0000	0.5000	2.0000	0.5000	1.0000	1.0000	2.0000	1.0000	0.5000	1.0000	0.5000	0.3333	0.5000	1.0000	0.3333	A_3
C_2	A_1	3.0000	4.0000	2.0000	3.0000	1.0000	3.0000	4.0000	0.5000	4.0000	2.0000	3.0000	2.0000	3.0000	5.0000	3.0000	2.0000	4.0000	2.0000	5.0000	3.0000	4.0000	3.0000	A_2
	A_2	1.0000	0.5000	1.0000	1.0000	0.5000	0.3333	0.5000	1.0000	0.3333	0.5000	1.0000	0.2500	0.5000	2.0000	1.0000	0.2500	2.0000	0.3333	0.5000	1.0000	2.0000	0.5000	A_3
C_3	A_1	4.0000	2.0000	5.0000	3.0000	4.0000	3.0000	3.0000	4.0000	2.0000	5.0000	3.0000	3.0000	5.0000	2.0000	1.0000	3.0000	4.0000	0.5000	4.0000	2.0000	3.0000	2.0000	A_2
	A_2	2.0000	0.3333	0.5000	1.0000	2.0000	0.5000	2.0000	0.5000	1.0000	3.0000	0.3333	0.5000	0.5000	0.2500	0.5000	0.3333	0.5000	1.0000	0.3333	0.5000	1.0000	0.2500	A_3
C_4	A_1	2.0000	5.0000	2.0000	4.0000	2.0000	5.0000	3.0000	4.0000	3.0000	3.0000	4.0000	2.0000	2.0000	5.0000	3.0000	4.0000	0.5000	4.0000	2.0000	3.0000	2.0000	4.0000	A_2
	A_2	0.3333	0.5000	0.2500	2.0000	0.3333	0.5000	1.0000	2.0000	0.5000	2.0000	0.5000	1.0000	0.3333	0.5000	0.3300	0.5000	1.0000	0.3333	0.5000	1.0000	0.2500	2.0000	A_3
C_5	A_1	5.0000	2.0000	2.0000	3.0000	2.0000	4.0000	2.0000	5.0000	3.0000	4.0000	3.0000	3.0000	3.0000	1.0000	1.0000	3.0000	4.0000	1.0000	4.0000	2.0000	3.0000	2.0000	A_2
	A_2	2.0000	0.3333	0.5000	1.0000	0.2500	2.0000	0.3333	0.5000	1.0000	2.0000	0.5000	2.0000	1.0000	0.5000	0.5000	0.3333	0.5000	1.0000	0.3333	0.5000	1.0000	0.2500	A_3
C_6	A_1	4.0000	3.0000	3.0000	4.0000	1.0000	3.0000	4.0000	0.5000	4.0000	2.0000	3.0000	2.0000	2.0000	5.0000	4.0000	2.0000	3.0000	2.0000	4.0000	2.0000	5.0000	3.0000	A_2
	A_2	2.0000	0.5000	2.0000	0.5000	0.5000	0.3300	0.5000	1.0000	0.3333	0.5000	1.0000	0.2500	0.3333	0.5000	0.3333	0.5000	1.0000	0.2500	2.0000	0.3333	0.5000	1.0000	A_3
C_7	A_1	4.0000	3.0000	3.0000	1.0000	3.0000	4.0000	0.5000	4.0000	2.0000	3.0000	2.0000	3.0000	2.0000	3.0000	2.0000	4.0000	2.0000	5.0000	3.0000	4.0000	3.0000	3.0000	A_2
	A_2	0.5000	0.5000	1.0000	0.5000	0.3333	0.5000	1.0000	0.3333	0.5000	1.0000	0.2500	1.0000	0.5000	1.0000	0.2500	2.0000	0.3333	0.5000	1.0000	2.0000	0.5000	2.0000	A_3
C_8	A_1	3.0000	4.0000	0.5000	4.0000	2.0000	3.0000	2.0000	4.0000	2.0000	5.0000	3.0000	4.0000	3.0000	4.0000	2.0000	4.0000	2.0000	5.0000	3.0000	3.0000	3.0000	1.0000	A_2
	A_2	0.3333	0.5000	1.0000	0.3300	0.5000	1.0000	0.2500	2.0000	0.3333	0.5000	1.0000	2.0000	0.3333	0.5000	0.2500	2.0000	0.3333	0.5000	1.0000	0.5000	1.0000	0.5000	A_3

Table 9.
The linguistic term with its corresponding number to the priority weight of three attractive FDI strategies.

		E_1	E_2	E_3	E_4	E_5	E_6	E_7	E_8	E_9	E_{10}	E_{11}	E_{12}	E_{13}	E_{14}	E_{15}	E_{16}	E_{17}	E_{18}	E_{19}	E_{20}	E_{21}	E_{22}	
C_1	A_1	0.7153	0.8413	0.7153	0.9307	0.7153	1.0000	0.8413	0.9307	0.8413	0.8413	0.9307	0.7153	0.9307	0.5000	0.7153	0.8413	0.8413	0.5000	0.8413	0.9307	0.2847	0.9307	A_2
	A_2	0.2847	0.5000	0.0693	0.7153	0.1587	0.2847	0.5000	0.7153	0.2847	0.7153	0.2847	0.5000	0.5000	0.7153	0.5000	0.2847	0.5000	0.2847	0.1587	0.2847	0.5000	0.1587	A_3
C_2	A_1	0.8413	0.9307	0.7153	0.8413	0.5000	0.8413	0.9307	0.2847	0.9307	0.7153	0.8413	0.7153	0.8413	1.0000	0.8413	0.7153	0.9307	0.7153	1.0000	0.8413	0.9307	0.8413	A_2
	A_2	0.5000	0.2847	0.5000	0.5000	0.2847	0.1587	0.2847	0.5000	0.1587	0.2847	0.5000	0.0693	0.2847	0.7153	0.5000	0.0693	0.7153	0.1587	0.2847	0.5000	0.7153	0.2847	A_3
C_3	A_1	0.9307	0.7153	1.0000	0.8413	0.9307	0.8413	0.8413	0.9307	0.7153	1.0000	0.8413	0.8413	1.0000	0.7153	0.5000	0.8413	0.9307	0.2847	0.9307	0.7153	0.8413	0.7153	A_2
	A_2	0.7153	0.1587	0.2847	0.5000	0.7153	0.2847	0.7153	0.2847	0.5000	0.8413	0.1587	0.2847	0.2847	0.0693	0.2847	0.1587	0.2847	0.5000	0.1587	0.2847	0.5000	0.0693	A_3
C_4	A_1	0.7153	1.0000	0.7153	0.9307	0.7153	1.0000	0.8413	0.9307	0.8413	0.8413	0.9307	0.7153	0.7153	1.0000	0.8413	0.9307	0.2847	0.9307	0.7153	0.8413	0.7153	0.9307	A_2
	A_2	0.1587	0.2847	0.0693	0.7153	0.1587	0.2847	0.5000	0.7153	0.2847	0.7153	0.2847	0.5000	0.1587	0.2847	0.1556	0.2847	0.5000	0.1587	0.2847	0.5000	0.0693	0.7153	A_3
C_5	A_1	1.0000	0.7153	0.7153	0.8413	0.7153	0.9307	0.7153	1.0000	0.8413	0.9307	0.8413	0.8413	0.8413	0.5000	0.5000	0.8413	0.9307	0.5000	0.9307	0.7153	0.8413	0.7153	A_2
	A_2	0.7153	0.1587	0.2847	0.5000	0.0693	0.7153	0.1587	0.2847	0.5000	0.7153	0.2847	0.7153	0.5000	0.2847	0.2847	0.1587	0.2847	0.5000	0.1587	0.2847	0.5000	0.0693	A_3
C_6	A_1	0.9307	0.8413	0.8413	0.9307	0.5000	0.8413	0.9307	0.2847	0.9307	0.7153	0.8413	0.7153	0.7153	1.0000	0.9307	0.7153	0.8413	0.7153	0.9307	0.7153	1.0000	0.8413	A_2
	A_2	0.7153	0.2847	0.7153	0.2847	0.2847	0.1556	0.2847	0.5000	0.1587	0.2847	0.5000	0.0693	0.1587	0.2847	0.1587	0.2847	0.5000	0.0693	0.7153	0.1587	0.2847	0.5000	A_3
C_7	A_1	0.9307	0.8413	0.8413	0.5000	0.8413	0.9307	0.2847	0.9307	0.7153	0.8413	0.7153	0.8413	0.7153	0.8413	0.7153	0.9307	0.7153	1.0000	0.8413	0.9307	0.8413	0.8413	A_2
	A_2	0.2847	0.2847	0.5000	0.2847	0.1587	0.2847	0.5000	0.1587	0.2847	0.5000	0.0693	0.5000	0.2847	0.5000	0.0693	0.7153	0.1587	0.2847	0.5000	0.7153	0.2847	0.7153	A_3
C_8	A_1	0.8413	0.9307	0.2847	0.9307	0.7153	0.8413	0.7153	0.9307	0.7153	1.0000	0.8413	0.9307	0.8413	0.9307	0.7153	0.9307	0.7153	1.0000	0.8413	0.8413	0.8413	0.5000	A_2
	A_2	0.0693	0.7153	0.1587	0.2847	0.5000	0.2847	0.5000	0.2847	0.1587	0.2847	0.5000	0.1556	0.2847	0.5000	0.0693	0.7153	0.1587	0.2847	0.5000	0.7153	0.5000	0.2847	A_3

Table 10.
The transformed fuzzy preference value of three attractive FDI strategies.

C_1	A_1	A_2	A_3
A_1	0.5000	0.7775	0.6766
A_2	0.2225	0.5000	0.3991
A_3	0.3234	0.6009	0.5000
Total	1.0459	1.8784	1.5757

Table 11.
Aggregated pairwise comparison matrices 22 evaluator of C_1.

C_1	A_1	A_2	A_3	Total	Average
A_1	0.4781	0.4139	0.4294	1.3214	0.4405
A_2	0.2127	0.2662	0.2533	0.7322	0.2441
A_3	0.3092	0.3199	0.3173	0.9464	0.3155
Total				3.0000	1.0000

Table 12.
Normalized matrix of priority weight of C_1.

	Weight	Priority			Weighted rate		
		A_1	A_2	A_3	A_1	A_2	A_3
C_1	0.2022	0.4405	0.2441	0.3155	0.0891	0.0494	0.0638
C_2	0.1529	0.4396	0.2333	0.3271	0.0672	0.0357	0.0500
C_3	0.1139	0.4378	0.2292	0.3330	0.0499	0.0261	0.0379
C_4	0.1551	0.4427	0.2238	0.3335	0.0687	0.0347	0.0517
C_5	0.1083	0.4290	0.2367	0.3343	0.0465	0.0256	0.0362
C_6	0.1227	0.4318	0.2336	0.3446	0.0530	0.0274	0.0423
C_7	0.0738	0.4366	0.2321	0.3112	0.0322	0.0171	0.0245
C_8	0.0710	0.4354	0.2347	0.3399	0.0309	0.0160	0.0241
Total	1.0000				0.4374	0.2320	0.3306

Table 13.
Normalized matrix of priority weight of all criteria and preference rate of candidates.

attract FDI for developing supporting industries is one that motivates Vietnam's economy's sustainable growth.

6. Conclusions

This study interviewed approximately 22 policy-makers, economists, and managers to identify their individual prioritization of the goals and assessment criteria discussed above. Based on the opinions of all survey respondents, the following findings were obtained:

"Institutions and policies" is the most important criterion considered by supporting industries in attracting potential FDI. Because Vietnam has joined the AFTA, the WTO, and the CPTPP, the Vietnamese government must now concentrate on building special policies for the promotion of supporting industries, which will involve legal, institutional, and policy-driven changes and improvements consistent with membership in such global trade organizations.

Domestic supply capacity, human resources, technological development and innovation, infrastructure facilities, and market size of the supporting industries have also received heavier weightings in selecting a strategy for attracting FDI. Notably, international cooperation and competition, along with other outstanding criteria, are not presently taken in terms of seriousness, which will undoubtedly lead to diminished levels of future FDI.

All survey evaluators agreed that "attracting FDI for developing supporting industries, which motivates the economy's sustainable growth," is the best strategy to pursue for attracting FDI related to the development of Vietnam's supporting industries. This is followed by "attracting FDI for developing supporting industries, which stimulates the national technological development." The statement that ranked last was "attracting FDI for developing supporting industries, which increases national competitiveness."

The multi-criteria decision-making model for selecting a strategy attractive to FDI presented here is clearly applicable to the evaluation process. The proposed strategy also reveals the concerns and preferences of all supporting industries and main industries. The results of this study provide a valuable reference for the Vietnamese government and policy-makers useful to improve institutions and policies, domestic supply capacity, human resources, technological development and innovation, infrastructure facilities, and assistance to improve the environment for investment. The overall purpose is to better attract FDI that will lead to the development of supporting industries and to select the best strategy for attracting future FDI that will also develop the all-important, requisite supporting industries of Vietnam.

Together, based on these available results, we are continuing to produce future research via a large-scale survey in an effort to select a strategy for better developing supporting industries in Vietnam.

Acknowledgements

The authors would like to thank the reviewers for their constructive comments related to this article.

Conflicts of interest

The author declares no conflict of interest.

Author contributions

Nguyen Xuan Huynh designed the research and methodology. Nguyen Xuan Huynh and Hoang Dinh Phi collected and analyzed the data. Nguyen Xuan Huynh and Hoang Dinh Phi wrote and revised the paper and corrected the final manuscript.

Author details

Nguyen Xuan Huynh* and Hoang Dinh Phi
Hanoi School of Business and Management, Vietnam National University, Hanoi, Vietnam

*Address all correspondence to: huynhngx@gmail.com

References

[1] VDF, JICA. Survey Compares Context, Policy Measures and Results Developing Supporting Industries in ASEAN. Hanoi: Publisher Transport; 2011

[2] Chau N-V et al. Supporting Industries: Experience from Other Country and Solution for Vietnam. Hanoi, Vietnam: Information and Communication Publisher; 2010. pp. 43-323. (Part 2)

[3] Keller W, Yeaple S. Multinational enterprises international trade and productivity growth: Firm-level evidence from the United States. The Review of Economic and Statistics. 2009;**91**(4):821-831

[4] Herman E. Implications of aggregate demand on employment: Evidence from the Romanian economy. The Young Economists Journal. 2011;**16**:132-143

[5] Borensztein E, De Gregorio J, Lee J-W. How does foreign direct investment affect economic growth? Journal of International Economics. 1998;**45**:115-135

[6] Wang T-C, Wang C-N, Nguyen XH. Evaluating the influence of criteria to attract foreign direct investment to develop supporting industries in Vietnam by utilizing fuzzy preference relations. Sustainability. 2016;**8**(5):447

[7] Chau N-V et al. The Development Policy of Supporting Industries in Vietnam until 2020: The Report Topic at the State Level. Hanoi: Information and Communication; 2010. pp. 10-42. (Part 1)

[8] General Statistics Office of Vietnam (GSO). Statistical Handbook of Vietnam 2016. Hanoi, Vietnam: Statistics Publishing House; 2016

[9] Herrera-Viedma E, Herrera E, Chiclana F, Luque M. Some issues on consistency of fuzzy preference relations. European Journal of Operational Research. 2004;**154**:98-109

[10] Chang T-H, Hsu S-C, Wang T-C. A propose model for measuring the aggregative risk degree of implementing an RFID digital campus system with the consistent fuzzy preference relations. Applied Mathematical Modelling. 2013; **37**:2605-2622

[11] Chang T-H, Wang T-C. Measuring the success possibility of implementing advanced manufacturing technology by utilizing the consistent fuzzy preference relations. Expert Systems with Applications. 2009;**36**:4313-4320

[12] Chen Y-H, Chao R-J. Supplier selection using consistent fuzzy preference relations. Expert Systems with Applications. 2012;**39**:3233-3240

[13] Wang T-C, Chang T-H. Forecasting the probability of successful knowledge management by consistent fuzzy preference relations. Expert Systems with Applications. 2007;**32**:801-813

[14] Wang T-C, Chang T-H. Application of consistent fuzzy preference relations in predicting the success of knowledge management implementation. European Journal of Operational Research. 2007; **182**:1313-1329

[15] Wang T-C, Chen Y-H. Applying consistent fuzzy preference relations to partnership selection. Omega. 2007;**35**: 384-388

[16] Wang T-C, Lin Y-L. Applying the consistent fuzzy preference relations to select merger strategy for commercial banks in new financial environments. Expert Systems with Applications. 2009;**36**:7019-7026

[17] Ohno K. The Supporting Industry, some Analyses and Consideration.

VDF&GRIPS; 2004 [Accessed: 10 April 2018]

[18] Ohno K. Supporting in Vietnam from the Perspective of Japanese Manufacturing Firms. VDF&GRIPS; 2006 [Accessed: 10 April 2018]

[19] The Prime Minister. Approval scheme, Help Developing Small and Medium Enterprises in Supporting Industries Field. No. 1556/QD-TTg. Hanoi, Vietnam: The Prime Minister; 2012 [Accessed: 10 April 2018]

[20] Ministry of International Trade and Industry (MITI). Keizai Kyouryoku Hakusho (White Paper on Economic Cooperation). Tokyo, Japan: MITI; 1985

[21] The Prime Minister. On Development Policies of Some Supporting Industries. No. 12/2011/QD-TTg. Hanoi, Vietnam: The Prime Minister; 2011 [Accessed: 10 April 2018]

[22] The Prime Minister. On Promulgating List of Supporting Industry Products Which Are Given Priority for Development. No. 1843/QĐ-TTg. Hanoi, Vietnam: The Prime Minister; 2011 [Accessed: 10 April 2018]

[23] Ichikawa K. Building and Strengthening Supporting Industries in Vietnam: A Survey Report. Hanoi, Vietnam: JETRO; 2005

[24] Porter M-E. The Competitive Advantage of Nations. New York: Free Press; 1990

[25] Communist Party of Vietnam. Resolutions of the 12th Congress of the Party of Vietnam. Hanoi, Vietnam: Communist Party of Vietnam; 2016 [Accessed: 10 April 2018]

[26] Communist Party of Vietnam. Resolutions of the 11th Congress of the Party of Vietnam. Hanoi, Vietnam: Communist Party of Vietnam; 2011 [Accessed: 10 April 2018]

[27] Communist Party of Vietnam. Resolutions of the 10th Congress of the Party of Vietnam. Hanoi, Vietnam: Communist Party of Vietnam; 2006 [Accessed: 10 April 2018]

[28] Communist Party of Vietnam. Resolutions of the 9th Congress of the Party of Vietnam. Hanoi, Vietnam: Communist Party of Vietnam; 2001 [Accessed: 10 April 2018]

[29] The Minister of Industry and Trade. Approving the Planning of Industrial Development Supports up to 2010 and Vision to 2020. No. 34/2007/QD-BCN. Hanoi, Vietnam: The Minister of Industry and Trade; 2007 [Accessed: 10 April 2018]

[30] The Minister of Industry and Trade. Approval Master Plan for Developing Supporting Industries up to 2020, Vision to 2030. No. 9028/QD-BCT. Hanoi, Vietnam: The Minister of Industry and Trade; 2014 [Accessed: 10 April 2018]

[31] The Prime Minister. On the Development of Supporting Industries. No. 1111/2015/ND-CP. Hanoi, Vietnam: The Prime Minister; 2015 [Accessed: 10 April 2018]

[32] The Prime Minister. On the Approving of the Program On Development Of Supporting Industries from 2016 to 2025. No. 68/QD-TTg. Hanoi, Vietnam: The Prime Minister; 2017 [Accessed: 10 April 2018]

[33] The Prime Minister. Promulgating the Regulation on Management and Implementation of the Program on Development of Supporting Industries. No. 10/2017/QD-TTg. Hanoi, Vietnam: The Prime Minister; 2017 [Accessed: 10 April 2018]

[34] The Minister of Industry and Trade. Promulgating the Regulation on Formulation, Receipt, Appraisal,

Approval and Implementation of Schemes under the Program on Development of Supporting Industries. No. 4572/QD-BCT. Hanoi, Vietnam: The Minister of Industry and Trade; 2017 [Accessed: 10 April 2018]

[35] Industrial Policy and Strategy Institute. Overall Policy Developing Supporting Industries in Terms of Integration. Industrial Policy and Strategy Institute: Hanoi, Vietnam; 2010

[36] Vietnam Government. Vietnam Government Report: The Implementation of Socio-Economic Development in 2016. Vietnam Government: Hanoi, Vietnam; 2016 [Accessed: 10 April 2018]

[37] Mori J. Development of Supporting Industries for Vietnam's Industrialization Increasing Positive Vertical Externalities through Collaborative Training. Tufts University, London: The Fletcher School; 2005

[38] Crespo N, Fontoura M-P. Determinant factor of FDI spillovers: What do we really know? World Development. 2007;**35**(3):410-425

[39] Mihaela K. The relevance of foreign direct investment for sustainable development: Empirical evidence from European Union. Procedia Economics and Finance. 2014;**15**:1349-1354

[40] Ohno K, Hanoi National Graduate Institute for Policy Studies (GRIPS), Vietnam Development Forum (VDF). Building Supporting Industries in Vietnam. Vol. 1. Hanoi, Vietnam: Vietnam Development Forum; 2007

[41] Groh AP, Wich M. Emerging economies' attraction of foreign direct investment. Emerging Markets Review. 2012;**13**:210-229

[42] Danciu AR, Strat VA. Factors influencing the choice of the foreign direct investments locations in the Romanian regions. Procedia - Social and Behavioral Sciences. 2014;**109**:870-874

[43] Center Institute of Economic Management (CIEM). Subcontracting and Outsourcing, Economic Linkage between Large and Small Enterprises: Dispute Settlement and Contract Implementation. Hanoi, Vietnam: Central Institute of Economic Management; 2004

[44] Saaty T-L. Fundamentals of Decision Making and Priority Theory with the AHP. Pittsburgh: RWS Publications; 1994

[45] Saaty T-L. The Analytic Hierarchy Process: Planning, Priority Setting, Resources Allocation. London: McGraw-Hill; 1980